Ticonderoga 1758

Montcalm's victory against all odds

OSPREY
PUBLISHING

Ticonderoga 1758

Montcalm's victory against all odds

René Chartrand · Illustrated by Patrice Courcelle

Series editor Lee Johnson • Consultant editor David G Chandler

First published in Great Britain in 2000 by Osprey Publishing, Elms Court,
Chapel Way, Botley, Oxford OX2 9LP, United Kingdom
Email: info@ospreypublishing.com

© 2000 Osprey Publishing Ltd.

Reprinted 2002, 2003

CIP Data for this publication is available from the British Library

ISBN 1 84176 093 5

Editor: Marcus Cowper
Design: Ken Vail Graphic Design, Cambridge, UK

Colour bird's eye view illustrations by the Black Spot
Cartography by The Map Studio
Battlescene artwork by Patrice Courcelle
Originated by Grasmere Digital Imaging, Leeds, UK
Printed in China through World Print Ltd

03 04 05 06 10 9 8 7 6 5 4 3

FOR A CATALOGUE OF ALL BOOKS PUBLISHED BY
OSPREY MILITARY AND AVIATION PLEASE CONTACT:

The Marketing Manager, Osprey Direct UK,
PO Box 140, Wellingborough, Northants,
NN8 2FA, United Kingdom.
Email: info@ospreydirect.co.uk

The Marketing Manager, Osprey Direct USA,
c/o MBI Publishing, PO Box 1,
729 Prospect Avenue, Osceola, WI 54020, USA.
Email: info@ospreydirectusa.com

www.ospreypublishing.com

Dedication

To the memory of Stephen H. P. Pell (1874–1950).

Acknowledgments

In the preparation of this volume, Col. Ian McCulloch of the
History and Heritage Directorate at the Canadian
Department of National Defense most generously shared
the results of his research on the 1758 campaign, as well
as his outlook on its results which, as a whole, I fully share.
Curators Christopher D. Fox at the Fort Ticonderoga
Museum and Peter Harrington of the Anne S.K. Brown
Military Collection at Brown University kindly assisted on
visual material. Last but not least, Osprey editor Marcus
Cowper who turned it all into a handy and visually pleasing
volume. To one and all, please accept my heartfelt
expression of deepest gratitude.

Artist's Note

Readers may care to note that the original paintings from
which the colour plates in this book were prepared are
available for private sale. All reproduction copyright
whatsoever is retained by the publisher. All enquiries
should be addressed to:

Patrice Courcelle, 33 Avenue des Vallons. 1410 Waterloo,
Belgium.

The publishers regret that they can enter into no
correspondence on this matter.

KEY TO MILITARY SYMBOLS

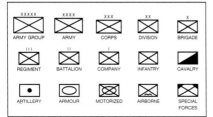

FRONT COVER:
**Montcalm cheered by his troops
following the final repulse of the
British assaults on 8 July 1758.
Many of the uniform details
are erroneous in this
early-20th-century painting by
Henry Ogden, but it captures
marvelously well the elation in
the French camp after the battle.
(Fort Ticonderoga Museum)**

CONTENTS

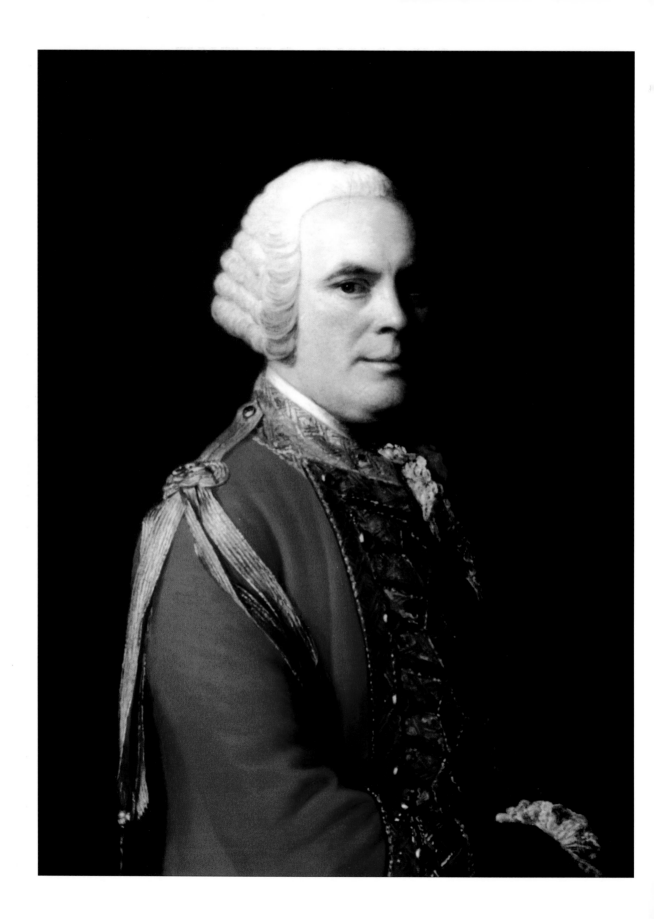

ORIGINS OF THE CAMPAIGN

TICONDEROGA: **SETTING AND HISTORY**

"Carillon" – that is the name by which Montcalm's greatest victory is known in the francophone world. To Americans and Britons, it is "Ticonderoga". Both words, Carillon and Ticonderoga, conjure up epic deeds and acts of heroism performed by many thousands of men during an incredible day-long battle in the primeval North American wilderness.

Ticonderoga is the Indian name of the area which was controlled by the Mohawk Indians, one of the nations of the powerful Iroquois confederation. Its French name of Carillon is said to have been given

because of the nearby waterfalls of the La Chute River, whose sound rang out like church bells. Ticonderoga is situated on the southern side of a peninsula which separates Lake Champlain from the much smaller Lake George to the south. The lakes are connected by the La Chute River.

The first European party to explore the area of Ticonderoga was led by Samuel de Champlain in 1609. Having founded Quebec the previous year, he traveled south with two French companions and a host of Indian allies in an armada of canoes. Landing at the southern end of Lake Champlain, Champlain and his party met a large war party of Iroquois. On 30 July, both sides faced each other when Champlain appeared in armor with an arquebus aimed at the startled Iroquois. His first shot, loaded with four balls, downed two chiefs and spread panic among the Iroquois. His two French companions, hidden from view, now opened fire. The engagement set the Iroquois against the French for decades to come. That same year, 1609, Henry Hudson was exploring what became the Hudson River. The Dutch later built settlements along its shores, while various colonies were founded along the Atlantic seaboard by waves of settlers from Britain during the 17th and early-18th centuries.

By the middle of the 18th century, North America was divided between France and Great Britain. As can be seen in the first map, the French domain, New France, was enormous, while the British New England was limited to the eastern seaboard. French explorers ventured further into the interior of North America. They explored the Great Lakes and were, for nearly a century, the sole Europeans to have forts and missions in that area. By 1682 they had reached the Gulf of Mexico, and New France formed an enormous arc right across North America. But as impressive as it may have looked on a map, New France remained a weak colony in terms of population. By the middle of the 18th century, there were only about 70,000 inhabitants of European origin, while the 13 colonies of New England boasted about a million-and-a-half. The population of the Indian nations had decreased considerably during the

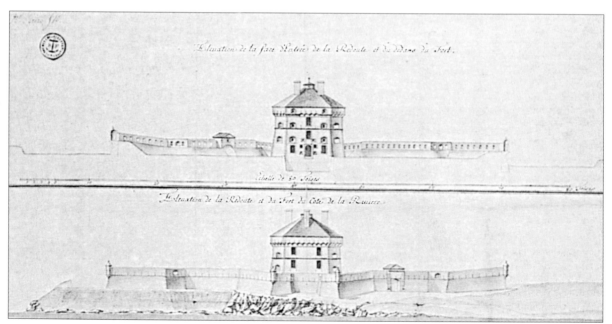

17th century because of their exposure to European diseases and no accurate population figure is known.

STRATEGIC IMPORTANCE

New France and New England were separated by vast forests and mountain ranges. The Six Nations Iroquois, allied to the British, were the true rulers of the Mohawk Valley, north of Albany, up to Lake Champlain. There was a traditional invasion route through the wilderness – the Lake George–Lake Champlain–Richelieu River route – first used by the Mohawks to raid the French settlements. To protect themselves, the French built forts along the Richelieu River, Chambly and Saint-Jean being the most important in the early-18th century. By then, however, the tables had turned and the men of French Canada had gained the upper hand thanks to their extraordinary mastery of raid warfare. Some of the Iroquois had become allies of the French and formed four of the Seven Nations (or Lodges) of Canada, the others being the Abenakis, the Algonquin and the Hurons who settled in the St Lawrence Valley.

In an attempt to provide a forward base, as well as an early warning against invasion, Beauharnois, the governor-general of New France,

THE SITUATION IN NORTH AMERICA, 1758

HUDSON BAY

RUPERT'S LAND

HUDSON'S BAY COMPANY

F R A N C E

NEWFOUNDLAND

Gulf of
St Lawrence

St Lawrence

Lake Superior

C A N A D A

Île
St Jean

ACADIA

Île Royale
Louisbourg

Quebec

Montreal

Halifax
NOVA
SCOTIA

Lake
Michigan

Lake
Huron

Frontenac

Ticonderoga

Lake Ontario

Niagara

Detroit

Lake Erie

Albany

Boston

N E W

Ohio

New York
Philadelphia

BRITISH
13 COLONIES

Ohio

Williamsburg

L O U I S I A N A

Mississippi

ATLANTIC
OCEAN

New Orleans

FLORIDA

GULF OF MEXICO

N

BAHAMA
ISLANDS

CUBA

HISPANOLIA

MEXICO

HAITI

	Britain
	France
	Spain
	Disputed
←	British attacks

| 0 | | 250 miles |
| 0 | | 400 km |

Fort Saint-Frédéric's stone foundations as seen today, looking north, with Lake Champlain in the background. Fort Saint-Frédéric was blown up in 1759 by the retreating French. (Photo: RC)

ordered the construction of a fort in 1731 at Pointe-à-la-Chevelure (Scalp Point, or Crown Point, to the British and New Englanders). Over the next few years, an imposing stone structure went up which became known as Fort Saint-Frédéric. It effectively secured Lake Champlain and proved extraordinarily useful to the French during the War of the Austrian Succession (1744–48) when the French were able to raid the borders of the British colonies in the south.

On their side, the English colonists had built settlements at Old Saratoga (now Schuylerville, NY) and Fort Lydius, which were both destroyed by Canadian raiding parties during the 1740s. Tensions were such between New France and New England in the early 1750s that, by 1755, a state of war broke out between the two colonies. Regiments were sent from Britain and France to reinforce their respective colonies and the first campaigns of the Seven Years War, formally declared in 1756, were undertaken in the American wilderness on several fronts by the numerically superior Anglo-Americans.

OPPOSING PLANS

FORT CARILLON

On the Lake George–Lake Champlain front, an army of New Englanders under the colonial Gen. William Johnson resolved to take Fort Saint-Frédéric in 1755. Marching up from Albany, the New Englanders built a new fort named Fort Edward on the site of Lydius. It was to prove a most useful base then and in the years to follow. They moved further north to the southern shore of Lake George. On 8 September a powerful French force, which included two metropolitan army battalions, attacked Johnson and his colonials. Gen. Dieskau commanding the French forces made a European-style frontal attack on the entrenched New Englanders, however, which failed miserably. Dieskau was wounded and captured in the battle, and the New

Mid-18th-century iron naval cannon marked with a *fleur de lys* and letters. This piece of ordnance was brought to the fort between 1756 and 1758. The carriage should be red with black ironwork. (Photo: RC)

Michel Chartier de Lobtinière (1723–98) was the young engineer officer who laid out the plans for Fort Carillon. Born in Canada and commissioned in the *Compagnies franches de la Marine*, he was noticed by Governor-General La Galissonière as a promising officer, and sent to France for further training, returning to Canada in 1753 as an engineer. His first big assignment was Fort Carillon for which he was bitterly criticized by Montcalm and his metropolitan engineer, Pontleroy, largely because he was a relative of Governor-General Vaudreuil. His fort at Ticonderoga had its faults, but it certainly gave the British plenty of trouble, as did his 1759–60 fortifications on Ile aux Noix. His military career ruined by Montcalm's and Pontleroy's malignant gossip, Lobtinière nevertheless went on to further services, notably as a French diplomatic envoy to the American insurgents. His good services were finally recognized, largely thanks to Lévis who had risen to the rank of marshal, and Lobtinière was knighted in 1781 and ennobled a marquis in 1784. His Fort Carillon/Ticonderoga has certainly stood the test of time and is now one of the best-known heritage sites in the United States. (B. Sulte, Histoire des Canadiens-Français, Montreal, 1884)

Englanders quickly reinforced their position by building Fort William-Henry, a bastioned earth and timber work. They went no further and the campaign ended in a draw. Similarly, on 20 September, Governor-General Vaudreuil of New France ordered the construction of a fort at Ticonderoga to guard the northern tip of Lake George. A young colonial engineer, Michel de Lotbinière, was put in charge and work started in mid-October. By mid-1756, some 30 cannons were mounted in the bastioned fort and work continued for the next two years.

Governor-General Vaudreuil's strategy was basically the continuation of that used for over a half-century: to keep the British colonies along the eastern seaboard on the defensive by launching daring raids deep into their territory. Fort Carillon provided the most forward base on the vital Richelieu River–Lake Champlain–Lake George waterway, being even further south than Fort Saint-Frédéric at Crown Point. Fort Carillon soon proved to be a sharp thorn in the side of the Anglo-Americans. No settlers really felt safe north of Albany, or indeed in western Massachusetts or northern Connecticut, a fact which certainly helped to mobilize the New Englanders against the French. They had failed repeatedly in attempts to march on Crown Point. Now, an additional and substantial obstacle had been erected at Ticonderoga which was to quickly prove a formidable base for the French.

BRITISH INVASION STRATEGY

After Gen. Braddock's Anglo-American disaster on the Monongahela (9 July 1755) and a general stalemate elsewhere, James Campbell, Earl of Loudoun, was named British commander-in-chief in North America in 1756. Lord Loudoun's particular talent was strategy, and he soon discovered there was no coherent Anglo-American war plan. He therefore formulated an invasion strategy for the conquest of Canada that would be consistently followed for the rest of the war. It called for overwhelming forces to be deployed on three fronts: the Ohio Valley, the Champlain Valley, and the Fortress of Louisbourg leading to the St Lawrence River and Quebec. The final objective was Montreal, where all three armies on the three fronts would meet after vanquishing all other obstacles. Loudoun had correctly determined that it was Montreal and not Quebec that was the strategic and commercial key to New France. This grand strategy called for the capture of forts Duquesne, Niagara, Frontenac and La Présentation to the west; the fortresses of Louisbourg and Quebec to the east; and forts Carillon, Saint-Frédéric, Saint-Jean and Chambly in the south–north route from Lake George to Montreal.

Any comparison of British and French military policy in North America reveals the French weakness. The French government was reluctant to send great numbers of troops to the colonies, although Canada had received more reinforcements than anywhere else. No army battalions had been sent to the valuable West Indian colonies, and only two regiments went to India. On the other hand, hundreds of French battalions were being marched into Germany. Clearly, that was where the French court felt the important fighting would occur and gains could be made. With Prussia facing the combined forces of France, Austria and Russia, and with little to hope for from Britain and Hanover, the result seemed like a foregone conclusion. Canada could wait. However,

0   50 miles
0   100 km

N

Quebec

Trois Rivières

St Lawrence

C A N A D A

VAUDREUIL
Montréal

Fort Chambly

Saint-Jean

Richelieu

Isle-aux-Noix

Ottawa

St Lawrence

LÉVIS

Green
Mountains

MASSACHUSETTS
(MAINE)

La Présentation

MONTCALM
(4,200)

Lake
Champlain

Fort Frontenac

Adirondack
Mountains

End of June: French forces
gather at Ticonderoga

Fort Saint-Frédéric (Crown Point)
Fort Carillon (Ticonderoga)

8 July: Abercromby defeated

25 August: Bradstreet takes
Fort Frontenac, then retreats

Lake
Ontario

Lake
George

Fort Ann

NEW HAMPSHIRE

Oswego

William-Henry

Portsmouth

Fort Stanwix

Fort Edward

Connecticut

BRADSTREET
(3,500)

Mohawk

Saratoga

ABERCROMBY
(17,600)

Finger Lakes

Schenectady

Albany

MASSACHUSETTS

NEW YORK

June: British forces and New
England troops gather at Albany

Boston

Cape Cod

Catskill Mountains

Hudson

RHODE
ISLAND

CONNECTICUT

Newport

New Haven

Susquehanna

Delaware

Fort Hamilton

Long Island

Fort Augusta

PENNSYLVANIA

NEW
JERSEY

New York

ATLANTIC OCEAN

Fort Harris

ABOVE **Fort Carillon (or Ticonderoga), partly restored, as seen from an aerial photo taken in 1927.**

BELOW **Fort Carillon's western bastions, originally built from 1755 and restored in the 1920s. (Photo: RC)**

William Pitt, the new British prime minister, favored using Britain's superiority at sea to capture French colonies by deploying most of the British army overseas. Thus, more and more British regular regiments landed in North America, while the American militiamen were encouraged to mobilize into "provincial" regiments.

French reinforcements, although much less numerous than the British effort, also arrived in Canada with a new commanding general, the Marquis de Montcalm. In 1756 he led his troops to capture Fort Oswego on Lake Ontario. In 1757 he went south to Fort Carillon with his army and from there brought his troops against Fort William-Henry which fell to the French forces in July. Both of these actions were very damaging and upsetting to the British and Americans, but Montcalm could do no more than destroy the forts as the French lacked the manpower to hold them. Blamed for the lack of any major success in 1757, the British commander Lord Loudoun was recalled.

Far from being discouraged, the Anglo-Americans mustered more troops for a major assault on New France during 1758 in accordance with Lord Loudoun's strategic plan. Pitt ensured that ample resources in men and money were made available for the task. Some 12,000 troops led by Gen. Amherst would board a vast fleet and attack Fortress Louisbourg on Ile Royale (now Cape Breton Island). A smaller army of about 7,000 men was marching into the Ohio Valley under Gen. John Forbes, with Fort Duquesne as its objective. The main thrust of the Anglo-American assault was against Fort Carillon at Ticonderoga, the key to the Champlain Valley. To carry out this task, up to 17,000 men would assemble on the site of Fort William-Henry under Gen. James Abercromby, the new commander-in-chief.

OPPOSING LEADERS

THE BRITISH

James Abercromby (1706–81), the commander-in-chief in North America and general commanding the expedition against Fort Carillon, was born in Banffshire, Scotland, and entered the army as a young ensign in the 25th Foot in 1717. The next decades saw him rise in the Scottish political hierarchy, thanks to his brother-in-law, Lord Braco. By the late 1730s he was MP for Banffshire, King's Printer for Scotland and lieutenant-governor of Stirling Castle. In 1746 he became colonel of the 1st Foot (Royal Scots) and as deputy-quartermaster-general took part in the successful expedition against the French port of Lorient. In Flanders the following year, he was

George Augustus, Lord Viscount Howe, c. 1757. He is shown wearing the uniform of a typical regimental officer, either his own 55th Foot which was scarlet faced with green, gold buttons and lace, or the 60th which he previous commanded which was faced blue with silver lace.

wounded at Hulst and thereafter retired from active military duty until the eve of the Seven Years War when he became colonel of the 52nd (later 50th) Foot. When Lord Loudoun became commander-in-chief in North America in 1756, he appointed his close friend Abercromby his deputy with the rank of major-general and had his colonelcy transferred to the 44th Foot. The regiment was already in America and had lost its colonel at Monongahela in 1755.

Abercromby was an efficient second-in-command. He devoted himself to the administrative staff work of the army in North America, as well as to rebuilding his own battered 44th Foot. He found his new regiment "in want of many things" regarding both materials and morale. Abercromby obviously had an engaging and open manner which made him a popular senior staff officer, not only among the British, but also among the American officers and politicians. Governor Alexander Codden of New York and the powerful William Shirley of Massachusetts were charmed by him. When Loudoun was recalled for political reasons, Pitt appointed Abercromby to replace him. In political and diplomatic terms, it was a logical step as he was respected by the colonial leaders. In military terms, Abercromby seemed the best man to continue Loudoun's strategy for the conquest of Canada. However, for all his diplomatic manners, Abercromby's administrative and command record was uninspired if efficient. His personal battle experience was not extensive and was limited to regimental commands. As supreme commander in North America, he now had to prove that he had superior skills in both strategy and tactics as well as being an inspired battlefield commander – a tall order for any officer.

A brilliant young officer, **George Augustus, Viscount Howe** (1725–58), was second-in-command in Abercromby's army. He arrived in North America in 1757 as colonel commanding the 60th Foot (Royal Americans) but was appointed to the 55th Foot in September and promoted brigadier-general on 29 December 1757. His promotion was a wise one, as, in many ways, Howe had all the tactical talents Abercromby lacked. Lord Howe seems to have been an exceptionally gifted individual with an extraordinary charisma, and contemporary accounts praise his intelligence and ability as an officer. He was especially keen on training troops for the peculiar conditions of warfare in North America, and quickly perceived the tactical value of light infantry. He encouraged the formation of light infantry and ranger units, and tried to adapt uniforms and equipment to suit the North American terrain.

Thomas Gage (*c.* 1720–87) was born in Sussex, England, and was commissioned in the 62nd Foot. Having acted as Lord Albermarle's ADC in the 1740s, seeing action at Fontenoy and Culloden, he became lieutenant-colonel of the 44th Foot and arrived in America in 1755 with Gen. Braddock. Gage was noted as a good regimental commander, insisting on strict discipline, and was clearly brave, judging by his behavior at the Monongahela disaster. While serving under Lord Loudoun, Gage felt that a repeat of Braddock's defeat could be avoided if the British army had light infantry. Loudoun instructed him to recruit the new 80th Light Infantry, a regiment that Gage would command as colonel. In 1758, Gage was third in command seniority, and second after Lord Howe's death but his true role in the Ticonderoga campaign remains shrouded.

John Bradstreet (1714–74) has often been termed an American, but he was born at Annapolis Royal, Nova Scotia, in what is now Canada. He was commissioned in the 40th Foot in 1735 and had participated in several campaigns by the time he joined Abercromby's staff in 1758. By now a lieutenant-colonel, Bradstreet had been recruiting New England "battoemen" (river boatmen) and building boats for a projected expedition to Fort Frontenac. These efforts were redirected and expanded by Abercromby to encompass the attack on Ticonderoga. Bradstreet was to have a distinguished role in the campaign.

Abercromby's chief engineer was young **Lt. Matthew Clerk**, 27th Foot, who replaced the ailing John Montresor. He was assisted by lieutenants George Garth and Charles Rivez, both of the 60th Foot. Clerk was obviously an energetic and bright young man, esteemed by those who had met him, although he lacked experience. Although he was later blamed by Abercromby for providing bad intelligence which led to the disastrous attack (and has been repeatedly condemned by countless historians since), Clerk was far from the only officer to blame.

Maj. Gen. Louis-Joseph, Marquis de Montcalm, officer commanding the French forces at Ticonderoga. (National Archives of Canada, C27665)

THE FRENCH

Gen. Louis-Joseph, Marquis de Montcalm (1712–59), was born at the château of Candiac, a son of the old nobility of Provence, and, as early as age nine, was commissioned ensign in the Hainault infantry regiment. He served in the Rhineland during the Polish Succession War (1732–35), and was appointed an ADC to Lt. Gen. Marquis de La Fare in the expedition to Prague where he was wounded in 1741. In 1743, he became colonel of the Auxerrois Regiment. An exceptionally brave officer, he won the St Louis cross in the field in 1744, and was wounded and captured by the Austrians in the Franco-Spanish defeat at Piacenza in June 1746. Exchanged, promoted to brigadier in 1747, he was again wounded in the Italian Alps. Following the peace of 1748, his Auxerrois Regiment was incorporated into the Flandres Regiment in February 1749. Montcalm would have rightly

Brig. Gen. François Gaston, Chevalier de Lévis, the cool and efficient second-in-command of the French army at Ticonderoga.

Col. Louis-Antoine de Bougainville (1729–1811) was Montcalm's young, brilliant first ADC. Later destined to a place in history as an early explorer of the South Pacific, he was already an internationally recognized scientist and mathematician. With Montcalm, he was probably the only officer in Canada who had some access to officials near the pinnacle of power at the French court, held by the Marquise de Pompadour. His opinions about Canada were generally the same as Montcalm's, if slightly less vitriolic. (Print after a portrait taken later in life)

clamored for compensation and a month later, he was commissioned to raise a new heavy cavalry regiment to bear his name: Montcalm's Regiment. It was an exceptional event as very few regiments were raised in peacetime. Satisfactory as this may have been, it was expensive and Montcalm was not from the rich *grande noblesse*, so in 1753 he retired after 31 years of service, having participated in 11 campaigns and sustained five wounds. He kept the colonelcy of his cavalry regiment which he would occasionally inspect: a pleasant but sober life for a man in the prime of life.

Dieskau's capture at Lake George in 1755 meant that the Ministry of War had to find a replacement. No general on the active list wanted to go to Canada and the choice narrowed down to Montcalm, a mere brigadier, who was keen on the idea. For Montcalm, it meant a promotion to *maréchal de camps* (major-general), while the Minister of War, the Marquis d'Argenson, gained a brave, experienced officer who had seen much action. On the other hand, Montcalm had never held a post of high command. A good senior commander also had to be tactful and diplomatic. D'Argenson must have hoped that Montcalm would acquire these qualities. This was not to be. Montcalm was a man with a quick and very vindictive temper.

Montcalm landed in Quebec on 13 May 1756 and first went to Ticonderoga in July 1756 to see the new Fort Carillon and to fool the British as to the real objective of the campaign which was Oswego on the southern shore of Lake Ontario. By 29 July he had returned to Fort Frontenac from where his 3,000-strong army besieged and took Oswego (10–14 August). Although victorious, Montcalm objected to the strategic decisions made by his superior, Governor-General Vaudreuil. He immediately disliked Vaudreuil, judging his military and administrative talents to be minimal. In contrast to the calm and polite Vaudreuil, Montcalm was fiery, absolutely certain of his own preconceived opinions, and full of terribly disparaging comments which he freely and unrestrainedly emitted. He penned increasingly vindictive letters to his political superior, the minister of war. Vaudreuil responded by writing to *his* superior, the minister of the navy.

In 1757 Vaudreuil believed that a campaign on the Lake George front attacking Fort William-Henry would ruin the British invasion efforts via Lake Champlain. Montcalm, who felt a defensive stance was best, grudgingly complied and at the head of 6,000 men and 1,600 Indians, captured the fort (3–6 August), but it was followed by the controversial massacre of the prisoners by some Indians. It has been said that Montcalm could have easily marched further south, and captured Fort Edward only a day's march away, as Vaudreuil urged him to do. But this sort of daring warfare was unfamiliar to Montcalm and his metropolitan officers, who thought in more cautious traditional terms of marches and counter-marches with artillery, of being outflanked and fighting in line. Instead, Montcalm took his troops back to Ticonderoga. To his credit, Montcalm had already led two very successful sieges against badly outnumbered garrisons with no hope of relief. The 1758 campaign, thanks to Lord Loudoun's long-term strategic plan, would reverse the odds. It would be Montcalm's turn to defend himself against a much superior force.

The French army's second-in-command was **Brig. Gen. François-Gaston, Chevalier de Lévis** (1720–87). First commissioned in 1735, he fought in Prague during 1741–42, at Dettingen in 1743 and in many engagements in Germany during the War of Austrian Succession, where he distinguished himself as a cool-headed, brave and competent officer. In 1756 he sailed for New France. As second-in-command of the metropolitan troops in Canada, he dealt efficiently with purely military matters, earning the appreciation of both officers and enlisted men. Calm, diplomatic and liberal, he was the very opposite of his commander, which enabled him to remain on good terms with both Montcalm and Vaudreuil. He could see the corruption inherent in the colonial administration headed by Intendant Bigot, but he conceded that the metropolitans, too, could have their faults in colonial eyes. Lévis believed that nothing would be gained by vitriolic comments and bad manners. He felt that patience and understanding could improve most situations, and that the worst offenses were a matter for the law courts. Most of all, this pragmatic officer believed that French leadership in Canada should be united. Lévis' influence and diplomatic behavior helped to restore good relations between the metropolitan and colonial officers both before and after the battle of Ticonderoga.

François-Charles de Bourlamarque (1716–64) was an officer of the Dauphin Regiments and had campaigned in Flanders in the 1740s. He later did staff work, notably revising the infantry's manual of arms introduced in 1755. The following year he was promoted to colonel on the staff in Canada, was awarded the St Louis cross and sailed with Montcalm to Quebec. He was third in the chain of command of the metropolitan officers after Montcalm and Lévis. Somewhat unlucky on the battlefield, he was slightly wounded at the siege of Oswego in 1756, hit much more seriously in the shoulder at Ticonderoga in 1758, and was shot again, but not too seriously, at Sainte-Foy in 1760. Having commanded the hopelessly outnumbered force which blew up forts Carillon and Saint-Frédéric in 1759, he returned to France in 1760 and later became governor of Guadeloupe where he died in 1764. Observers regarded Bourlamarque as an efficient, no-nonsense, brave career officer who could be depended upon.

Nicolas Sarrebource de Pontleroy (1717–1802) was born in Marseilles, joined the army engineers in 1735, campaigned in Italy in 1744–45, and was named chief engineer in Canada in 1755. He first went to Louisbourg then joined Montcalm's staff. Both men were from Provence and they got along famously. Certainly a competent officer, de Pontleroy was not always as popular with other army engineer officers. As one later put it, the "darkness of his country [southern France] and the arbitrary manners of his temper could create difficulties." At Ticonderoga he left much of the actual work to Desandrouin, his talented assistant.

Jean-Nicolas Desandrouin (1729–92) was born in Verdun, entered the Beauce Regiment as a lieutenant in 1746 and went into the French corps of army engineers upon graduating with distinction from the Mézières academy in 1752. Sent to Canada in 1756, he was a most efficient engineer at the sieges of Oswego and William-Henry. He won the coveted St Louis cross for his outstanding role in the fortification and defense of the heights of Ticonderoga. He went on to further distinguished service after the Seven Years War and came back to North America in 1780 as chief engineer of Gen. Rochambeau's French army.

Pierre de Rigaud, Marquis de Vaudreuil (1698–1778), governor-general of New France from 1755 to 1760, was the first Canadian-born officer to rise to the top position. He was not present at the battle of Ticonderoga, but as commander-in-chief in New France, he determined strategy. From the outset in 1755, Vaudreuil had his doubts about the efficiency of metropolitan troops and generals in the North American environment. While a handful of colonial regulars, militiamen and Indian allies triumphed over Gen. Braddock's regular British redcoats on the Monongahela, Gen. Dieskau's French metropolitan troops were beaten back by New England militiamen at Lake George with Dieskau being captured as the ultimate humiliation. After such a poor performance, Vaudreuil wrote back to France stating there was no need to send another general. However, the French court disagreed, and Gen. Montcalm arrived in 1756. The two soon came to detest each other. Vaudreuil's strategy rested on the tested values of raid warfare, which had kept the far more numerous Anglo-Americans at bay since the end of the 17th century. He felt Canada's only chance was to keep the Anglo-Americans on the defensive as long as possible.

OPPOSING ARMIES

MONTCALM'S FRENCH AND CANADIAN ARMY

The French army assembled by Montcalm at Ticonderoga was small in numbers compared to its Anglo-American rival, but it was a well-organized force. Montcalm could rely on a group of really good experienced officers on his personal staff and commanding the battalions. His force consisted mostly of metropolitan troops detached to Canada from the land army in France. He also had detachments of regular colonial infantry and artillery. Canadian militiamen were not numerous and there were very few Indians.

Fusilier, La Sarre Regiment, 1757. (Musée de l'Armée, Paris)

ABOVE LEFT **Fusilier, Royal-Roussillon Regiment, 1759. (Royal Library, Madrid)**

ABOVE CENTER **Grenadier, Languedoc Regiment, 1759. The bearskin cap was not yet officially adopted for grenadiers in the French army, but several figures in this manuscript show it. It may have been worn by grenadiers in Canada, as bearskin was common enough. (Royal Library, Madrid)**

ABOVE RIGHT **Fusiliers, Berry Regiment, 1759. (Royal Library, Madrid)**

The metropolitan infantry were Montcalm's own and favorite troops. All eight battalions were now assembled at Ticonderoga. They consisted of the second battalions of the La Reine, Languedoc, Guyenne and Béarn regiments which had arrived in 1755, the second battalions of Royal-Roussillon and La Sarre which had arrived with Montcalm in 1756, and the second and third battalions of Berry which had arrived in 1757. There had been no reinforcements sent from France since then apart from a few scattered detachments and some recruits.

Each battalion dispatched in 1755 and 1756 had an establishment of 32 officers and 525 NCOs and privates divided into 13 companies, one of grenadiers and 12 of fusiliers. The grenadier company had 45 men and the fusilier companies 40 men each. Eight fusilier companies, four of La Reine and four of Languedoc, had been captured by Admiral Boscawen's Royal Navy vessel while in transit on the ships *Lys* and *Alcide* in June 1755, so on 28 January 1757 they were re-created by royal order. On 25 February of the same year, the six battalions in Canada had their establishments raised to 50 men per company. To these reinforcements were added a few specialist officers from the army's Royal Artillerie and the metropolitan engineers.

All this sounded admirable on paper, but recruits were sent to Canada in such small numbers that Montcalm's battalions were in fact slowly decreasing in strength. In general, French line infantry battalions had a standard organization throughout the army. In France, the number of companies per battalion were raised to 17 in 1756, but this was not applied to the battalions posted in Canada. Also, the two battalions of the Berry Regiment which landed at Quebec from 23 to 29 July 1757, were organized differently. They had originally been selected to go to India and had been reorganized into a battalion structure compatible with the troops of the French East India Company. However, their destination was changed and they sailed for Quebec instead of Pondicherry. Both of these battalions had nine companies, one of grenadiers and eight of fusiliers. They mustered 49 officers and 1,033 NCOs and privates when they left France, but an epidemic broke out on the voyage and only 913 men landed at Quebec, including 200 who were quite sick. They were frequently referred to as the first and second but were in fact the second and third battalions. Berry's enlisted men were, for the most part, raw young recruits with no military experience at all. Thus, while the battalions already in Canada had gained a fair amount of battle experience, this was not the case for the two battalions of Berry. Ticonderoga would be their baptism of fire.

Detachments, commonly called *piquets* by the French, were often drawn from the metropolitan battalions. They were generally the size of a company and often seem to have gathered some of the better non-grenadier soldiers into a light infantry role, or for special duties.

The situation of the regular Canadian colonial infantry, the *Compagnies franches de la Marine*, was not much better. They were named *"Compagnies franches"* because they were organized into independent companies, and *"de la Marine"* because they were under the Ministry of the Navy, the department responsible for the administration and defense of France's American dominions. Established in Canada since 1683, they were routinely called the *troupes de la colonie* (the colony's troops). The officer corps, the great majority of whom were born in Canada, formed an important part of the gentry in colonial society. Many Canadian officers were masters of the wilderness tactical warfare in North America. The NCOs and privates were recruited in France and usually settled in

Grenadier, 42nd Regiment of Foot (The Black Watch), 1750s. The 42nd Highlanders' grenadiers wore bearskin caps rather than miter caps. Watercolor by Cecil P. Lawson after David Morier. (Anne S.K. Brown Military Collection, Brown University. Ph. R. Chartrand)

Canada after their period of service. Most were accustomed to European-style garrison duties, but a proportion of the men became well versed in the intricacies of the wilderness. The regular colonial troops were often used as cadres for parties of Canadian militiamen and Indians. Since 1750 there was also a small corps of colonial artillery in Canada, the *Canonniers-Bombardiers*, which had two companies since March 1757, and were considered the elite of the colony's troops. At the beginning of the Seven Years War, the garrison of Canada had 30 infantry companies with an establishment of four officers and 50 men each. This had been augmented to 65 enlisted men by 14 March 1756, and the number of companies raised to 40 on 15 March 1757 giving a total of 2,600 men led by 160 officers. This was on paper, in Versailles. Such numbers were never actually seen in Canada and the number of colonial troops was, at very best, some 2,000 officers and men fit for service in 1758, about 1,200 of them in eastern Canada with the rest scattered across western outposts. The number at Ticonderoga may have been about 450 men divided into ten companies and probably included a strong colonial artillery component as it was headed by two captains.

The Canadian militia was a very different organization from the New England provincial troops. In Canada, every able-bodied man from 16 to 60 years of age was listed in his parish's company and was liable to a number of obligatory military and civic duties. In theory, militiamen going to war were to be volunteers, outstanding bush fighters familiar with woodcraft, while the less combatant militiamen would transport supplies. In practice, those better able to transport supplies were usually more numerous than the expert bush fighters. However, they made decent troops because, unlike most New England militiamen, the vast majority of Canadians learned to use hunting muskets in childhood (as did many Canadian girls).

The total number of militiamen on active duty tended to be much smaller than the number mustered. Canadian militiamen had no pay or uniforms, but were armed and equipped by the government when on duty. The militia was subject to central senior command by regular officers and, in that sense, was much less affected by political bickering than in New England and generally far better led than American provincial troops. Many were needed at home to grow crops and keep the economy going. In 1758 some 4,000 were called out, with 2,100 in eastern Canada and the rest mostly employed shipping supplies to garrisons in the Great Lakes and the west.

The Indians, especially the Iroquois of the Seven Nations of Canada, the traditional allies of the French, were not to be found in any numbers on the French side during the Ticonderoga campaign. Only 15 were recorded present on 8 July. This was partly due to Governor-General Vaudreuil's plan to raid New York via the Mohawk Valley. At the end of June, the Indians of the Seven Nations were waiting at the east end of Lake Ontario to be joined by Lévis and his men who were to come from Montreal. But Lévis went instead to Ticonderoga when it became clear that Abercromby was approaching. There was another, far more fundamental factor to explain the Indians' reluctance: the attitude of Montcalm and many of his metropolitan officers. The Indians loved Vaudreuil and the Canadian officers because they felt respected by them, but it is clear that Montcalm displayed little but scorn for them.

ABERCROMBY'S BRITISH AND NEW ENGLAND ARMY

For the campaign of 1758, the British and American forces in North America numbered about 44,000 officers and men. Of these, over 17,000 made up Abercromby's army marching on Ticonderoga.

British infantry regiments had only been numbered since 1751, so they were also identified by the older practice of using their colonel's name. Thus the 58th was also Howe's Regiment as Lord George Howe was its colonel. Each regiment usually had only one battalion divided into ten companies which included one of grenadiers. The number of men per battalion could vary considerably from one regiment to another, ranging from 500 men to over 1,000. The infantry regulars in Abercromby's army were, except for the newly raised 80th, all "regiments of Foot" denoting their status as line infantry. If their tactical purpose was identical, their origins were often different. The 27th, for example, was an Irish regiment as its name Inniskilling showed. The 60th was also exceptional in that it had four battalions, was partly recruited in North America, partly in continental Europe and largely led by Swiss and German officers. Six companies of its first battalion and its entire fourth battalion were with Abercromby. The most numerous was the 42nd Regiment which was recruited in the Highlands of Scotland. Its

ABOVE LEFT **Officer, 42nd Regiment of Foot, c. 1760. On 22 July 1758, the regimental facings were changed from buff to blue as the regiment became the Royal Highland Regiment. This illustration by A. E. Haswell Miller after an original painting is full of interesting details of early Highland regimental dress and armament. (*Journal of the Society for Army Historical Research*, 1940)**

ABOVE RIGHT **Private, 60th Foot (Royal Americans), 1755–67. The coats of the privates and corporals of this regiment had no lace. (Print after a reconstitution by P. W. Reynolds)**

2ᵈ Connecticut Regiment, 1760
Field Officer

ABOVE LEFT Officer, Grenadier Company, 60th Foot (Royal Americans), 1755–67. The officers and drummers of the 60th had their uniforms trimmed with lace. (Print after a reconstitution by P. W. Reynolds)

ABOVE RIGHT Officer, Col. Nathan Whiting's 2nd Connecticut Regiment, c. 1758–59. While most American provincial units wore blue, a few had red uniforms such as this Connecticut unit. Reconstitution by Herbert Knotel after an officer's portrait. (Anne S. K. Brown Military Collection, Brown University. Ph. R. Chartrand)

traditional dress was most distinctive and its armament featured broadswords and pistols as well as the muskets and bayonets carried by all infantrymen.

The 80th Regiment of Light Armed Foot was officially approved by the king on 5 May 1758 and Beating Orders were issued on 17 June at Kensington Palace. It was obvious the regular army needed a large light infantry unit in addition to the rangers. Lord Loudoun had advocated the formation of such a unit in late 1757 and had unofficially organized it in North America during the early part of 1758 under the command of Col. Thomas Gage. It had only five companies. Officers appointed to it remained on the rolls of their former units until official approval was received in America. The 80th was assigned brown uniforms with leather caps.

The six companies of rangers formed the other and most experienced corps of light troops with Abercromby's army. They were recruited from men familiar with woodcraft and the frontier in North America (two companies were made up of "Stockbridge" Indians) and were led by Maj. Robert Rogers, who was later to become something of a legendary figure. While the rangers were good scouts and courageous troops, they lacked discipline and their battle record was generally unfortunate against their French counterparts.

The artillery train, commanded by Capt. Thomas Ord, consisted of 18 guns, 13 mortars and 13 howitzers. There was a shortage of trained gunners so some 63 infantrymen were detached in the middle of June to join the 124 artillerymen. Abercromby therefore had adequate resources should he choose to besiege Fort Carillon.

American provincial troops made up the largest part of Abercromby's army. These were units distinct from the British regular army recruited every year in the various New England provinces, hence their name of "provincials". They have been called militias, but were actually recruited from militiamen who served from the spring to the fall. They were to be armed, paid, clothed and subsidized by their colony of origin. In the northeast, Massachusetts, Connecticut and New York contributed the most important contingents. The provincial troops were organized along the lines of the regulars, but generally without grenadier companies, most having one-battalion infantry regiments, although New York chose a three-battalion regiment structure. Some provinces also had rangers and light infantry, such as Putnam's Connecticut Ranger Company and Partridge's Massachusetts Light Infantry Regiment. In total the various colonies sent about 7,400 provincials.

Finally, some 1,600 armed "battoemen" were recruited to be part of the expedition. Often called provincials because they were Americans, they were enlisted under the same general conditions as provincials, but were subsidized by the crown. They were armed and paid, but had no uniform clothing. Many were familiar with navigating in the wilderness lakes and rivers, and were said to be even more ill-disciplined than the rangers, although improvements were made once Lt. Col. Bradstreet became their commander.

British commanders tried to adapt their arms, equipment and uniforms to suit warfare in the wilds of North America. The ten best marksmen in each regiment were issued with "rifled barreled guns" and practiced target shooting. In the 55th Foot, Lord Howe had the musket barrels shortened and blackened, forbade gold lace, had his soldiers' coat skirts cut short, had his own hair trimmed and ordered his troops to do the same. In late May 1758 Surgeon Richard Huck could write to a friend that Abercromby's army was one of "round heads", since everyone's hair was "an inch long", that tricorn brims had been cut to "two inches and a half broad", and the coat tails cut even "shorter than the Highlanders". The regular soldiers on the march were to "put their provisions in their haversacks and roll them up in their blankets like the rangers" and carry 36 rounds per man. Provincial troops do not appear to have followed these instructions to the letter as some of their clothing and equipment conformed already, while other measures such as cutting hair or hat brims seemed less necessary. In mid-May, Abercromby ordered that his officers would "not carry their sashes, but wear their gorgets on duty"; some even gave up their swords and wore tomahawks instead. Each officer was only to have "a soldier's tent, a small portemantle, blankets & bearskin." Finally, the regiments were ordered not to "carry their colours, nor camp colours to the field this campaigne."

ORDERS OF BATTLE

The orders of battle presented here are, of course, simplified and approximate as contemporary accounts vary, sometimes substantially, by hundreds and even thousands of men.

BRITISH ORDER OF BATTLE

Officer Commanding: Maj. Gen. James Abercromby

Brig. Gen. George Augustus, Lord Howe
Brig. Gen. Thomas Gage
Chief Engineer Matthew Clerk

27th Foot (Lord Blackeney's) 650 all ranks.
42nd Foot (The Black Watch – Lord John Murray's) 1,100 all ranks.
44th Foot (James Abercromby's) 850 all ranks.
46th Foot (Thomas Murray's) 650 all ranks.
55th Foot (Lord Howe's) 650 all ranks.
60th Foot (Royal Americans), 1st Bn. 550 and 4th Bn. 900 all ranks.
80th Light Armed Foot (Thomas Gage's) 350 to 450 all ranks.
Royal Artillery, two companies (Capt. John Thomas Ord) 125 all ranks with 44 pieces of ordnance.

Total British regulars: 5,825 all ranks.

Rogers' Rangers (Major Robert Rogers) four American companies – Rogers', Stark's, Burbank's and Shepperd's companies 300 men; two companies of Stockbridge Indians 100 men, for a total of 400 all ranks.
Col. Timothy Ruggle's Massachusetts Regiment 375 all ranks.
Col. Jonathan Bagley's Massachusetts Regiment 450 all ranks.
Col. Jedediah Preble's Massachusetts Regiment 525 all ranks.
Col. Joseph William's Massachusetts Regiment 470 all ranks.
Col. Oliver Partridge's Massachusetts Regiment (also termed battalion, organized as light infantry) 980 all ranks.

Col. Thomas Doty's (or Dotey's) Massachusetts Regiment 770 all ranks.
Col. Hineas Lyman's 1st Connecticut Regiment 500 all ranks.
Col. Nathan Whiting's 2nd Connecticut Regiment 475 all ranks.
Col. Elezaer Fitch's 3rd Connecticut Regiment 475 all ranks.
Col. David Wooster's 4th Connecticut Regiment 425 all ranks.
Major Israel Putnam's Connecticut Rangers 75 all ranks.
Col. Oliver De Lancey's New York Regiment between 1,300 and 1,700 all ranks.
1st Bn. Lt. Col. Bartholomew LeRoux
2nd Bn. Lt. Col. Melancthon Taylor Woolsey
3rd Bn. Lt. Col. Beamsley Glasier
Col. John Johnson's New Jersey Regiment 615 to 850 all ranks.
Col. Henry Babcock's Rhode Island Regiment 680 all ranks.
Col. John Hart's New Hampshire Regiment 610 all ranks.
Capt. Lovell's New Hampshire Rangers 90 all ranks.
Corps of Armed Battoemen (Lt. Col. John Bradstreet's) 1,600 all ranks.
Indians with Sir William Johnson, mostly Mohawks 400 warriors.

Total of American auxiliaries, provincials and Indians: 11,775.

Total of army: about 17,600.

FRENCH ORDER OF BATTLE

Officer Commanding: Maj. Gen. the Marquis de Montcalm

Brig. Gen. the Chevalier de Lévis
Col. de Bourlarmarque
Chief Engineer Nicolas Sarrebource de Pontleroy

La Reine (2nd Bn.) 345 all ranks.
Béarn (2nd Bn.) 410 all ranks.
Guyenne (2nd Bn.) 470 all ranks.
La Sarre (2nd Bn.) 460 all ranks.
Languedoc (2nd Bn.) 426 all ranks.
Royal-Roussillon (2nd Bn.) 480 all ranks.
Berry (2nd Bn.) 450 all ranks.
(3rd Bn.) Grenadier Company 50 men with 2nd Bn.; about 400 all ranks in Fort Carillon but of these an unknown number of men were detached to the heights to move supplies.

Canonniers-Bombardiers, probably about 50–60 men in the fort.
Compagnies franches de la Marine 150 and Canadian Militia 250 for a total of 400 all ranks. (This was later grudgingly revised by Montcalm to 451 at noon and to about 650 at 5 pm but the total by then was probably around 750 colonial infantrymen and militiamen.)
Indians 15 warriors

Total: about 4,200

THE CAMPAIGN

ABERCROMBY'S ARMY GATHERS

The instruction signed by William Pitt on 30 December 1757 arrived at Albany on 7 March 1758. The regulars now knew Abercromby was confirmed in command, and he knew he was to attack Ticonderoga. Couriers went out in the following days to the governors of New York, Massachusetts, Connecticut, New Jersey, New Hampshire and Rhode Island calling for some 20,000 provincial troops to be recruited and put on active service. The six northern colonies voted to raise 17,480 men which of course took some weeks; there were recruiting shortfalls in spite of decent bounties, and several colonies eventually resorted to compulsory drafts to fill the ranks.

The concentration point was Albany. British regular regiments gathered there, and from late May when the first contingents arrived from New York, they were joined by the provincials who would form the bulk of the army. By then, the gathering site had been moved closer to the southern tip of Lake George, to the site of Fort William-Henry destroyed by Montcalm the previous summer. Camp was set up from 19 June by the 42nd, 44th and 55th regiments, the New Jersey Regiment and the rangers led by Lord Howe. The logistical problems were substantial, with a lack of arms and camp equipage for the provincials being especially worrisome; it was only when 10,000 muskets and camp equipage for 4,000 men arrived in Albany from Britain (quite late) on 19 June that most provincials moved on to Lake George. Abercromby arrived in the last week of June, by which time the operation was finally coming together. Masses of supplies were being stockpiled, and about 1,000 bateaux and 200 whaleboats sent by Massachusetts were on the spot; Bradstreet's battoemen were preparing rafts for the artillery.

By the beginning of July, in spite of the substantial supply difficulties associated with assembling so many men, Abercromby and Howe stood at the head of some 17,000 men, the largest army ever assembled in North America. Scout reports indicated a much smaller number of French troops at Fort Carillon.

Private, Col. John Johnson's New Jersey Regiment, 1758. This regiment was nicknamed the "Jersey Blues" during the French and Indian War because of its uniform. The 1758 legislation called for a "blue coat, after the Highland manner, Lappel'd and cuffed with red, one pair of Ticken Breeches, one Blue ditto of the cloath as their Coat, one Check Shirt, one white ditto, two pairs yarn Stockings, two pairs of Shoes, one Hat to each Man, bound with yellow Binding, one Blanket, one Knapsack, one Hatchet, one Canteen, one Camp Kettle to five Men, a pair of white Spaterdashes," making it one of the better equipped American provincial regiments. Reconstitution by Herbert Knotel. (Anne S. K. Brown Military Collection, Brown University. Ph. R. Chartrand)

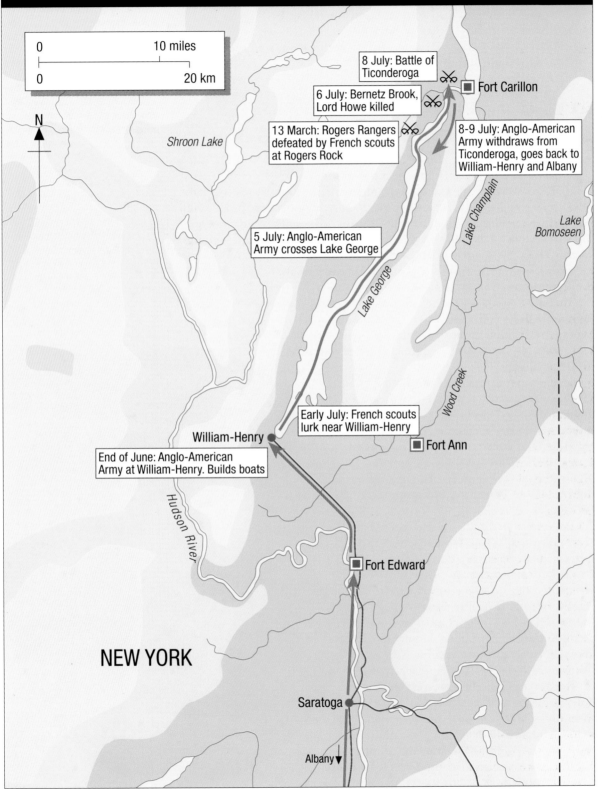

0

10 miles

0

20 km

N

Shroon Lake

8 July: Battle of Ticonderoga

6 July: Bernetz Brook, Lord Howe killed

13 March: Rogers Rangers defeated by French scouts at Rogers Rock

Fort Carillon

8-9 July: Anglo-American Army withdraws from Ticonderoga, goes back to William-Henry and Albany

Lake Champlain

Lake Bomoseen

5 July: Anglo-American Army crosses Lake George

Lake George

Wood Creek

Early July: French scouts lurk near William-Henry

William-Henry

End of June: Anglo-American Army at William-Henry. Builds boats

Fort Ann

Hudson River

Fort Edward

NEW YORK

Saratoga

Albany ▼

On 4 July, the British regiments were divided into three brigades:

1st Brigade under Lt. Col. William Haviland, 27th Foot: Blakeney's 27th Foot; six companies of the 1st Bn., 60th Foot; the complete 4th Bn., 60th Foot; two companies of the 80th Light Infantry.

2nd Brigade under Lt. Col. Francis Grant, 42nd Foot: Lord George Murray's 42nd Foot; Thomas Murray's 46th Foot; one company of the 80th Light Infantry.

3rd Brigade under Lt. Col. John Donaldson, 55th Foot: Abercromby's 44th Foot; Lord Howe's 55th Foot; two companies of 80th Light Infantry.

APPROACH OF ABERCROMBY'S TROOPS

On 5 July, Abercromby's army encamped at the south end of Lake George was in high spirits and ready to proceed. Hundreds of small craft were waiting to embark the troops and early that morning some 900 bateaux and 135 barges were filled with troops and supplies. The artillery was loaded on to a number of large flat-bottomed craft. In order to prevent confusion and to provide enough rowing space, the boats were arrayed in rows in an orderly fashion. The fleet of innumerable boats with their little white sails must have made an incredibly awesome sight: the armada moving up the lake was about a mile wide (1.8 km), (which was nearly the width of Lake George) and stretched for about seven miles (12 km) in length.

At the head of the fleet the rangers and the 80th Light Infantry formed the advance guard, followed by the British regular regiments which formed the center, the New England provincial troops on each side and the army's stores and supplies behind, with the artillery bringing up the rear. More light infantry formed a rear guard.

This extraordinary sight soon came into view of the French scouts. Ensign Jean-Baptiste Levrault de Langy's detachment of 130 men seems to have been the furthest south and was probably first to spot them. They went back at once to Ticonderoga to report to Montcalm. On the hills and mountains further north were two other large detachments of French troops: on the west side of the lake, 150 men mostly from La Reine with 100 volunteers from various regiments were at Roger's Rock under the command of Capt. de Trépezec. They kept the flotilla under surveillance from a safe distance and counted at least 700 boats. Another party of 300 men under

Lt. Col. Frederick Haldiman (1718–1791), 60th Foot, who led the British grenadiers during the battle. A very able Swiss officer in the British army, Haldiman rose to be governor-general of Canada during the later part of the American War of Independence, between 1778 and 1784. This portrait shows him in the uniform of a field officer of the 60th in the early 1770s.

Maj. Robert Rogers, the commander of the several companies of rangers at Ticonderoga. This French print credited him with being "Commander in Chief of Indian troops in American service," which was not quite the case. (National Archives of Canada, C6875)

LE MAJOR ROBERT ROGER
Commandant en Chef les Troupes Indiennes au service des Américains

Capt. Bernard was further back along Bernetz Brook to watch for enemy ranger parties which might try to outflank the French positions from the northwest.

At the top of Lake George, French sentry posts were dotted from the present Cook's Mountain to a camp at the beginning of the Portage Road. The agreed signal was to raise and lower a white flag when the British were fully in view. The sentries relayed the signal from post to post until Montcalm received word of the sightings and ordered the troops at the north end of the lake to withdraw.

The vast fleet of Anglo-American boats went as far as Sabbath Day Point, some 25 miles (40 km) to the north. The first division landed there in the late afternoon, while rangers and light infantry secured the area landing about two miles above. Tents and supplies were brought out of the bateaux and the army set up camp as darkness fell. Many fires were

On 5 July 1758, the French scouts on the mountains edging the northern end of Lake George beheld a truly grand and awesome sight: hundreds and hundreds of boats full of thousands of soldiers sailing up the lake. Ensign Langy and his party of colonial troops and militiamen were probably the first to see the boats. When on scouts in the woodlands, the colonial troops and militiamen wore moccasins and *mitasses* (Indian-style gaiters),

waistcoats or *capots* (the Canadian-style hooded coat) and sometimes the Indian breechclout rather than breeches. In the summer, Canadian militiamen preferred wearing just their shirts as shown in this plate. The colonial regulars might have worn tricorn hats, most likely the officers, or cloth caps as the militiamen. The soldiers carried military muskets with bayonets but militiamen usually preferred light-weight hunting muskets

with three knives, one hanging at the neck, another tucked in their waist sash and a smaller one at the mitasses garter. All carried tomahawks. Officers were to wear their gilded gorgets and colonial troops officers on scouts seem to have favored wearing their waistcoats. These were often edged with gold lace according to the inventories of belongings of Canadian *Compagnie franches* officers.

lit as the men cooked dinner and settled down for the night – or so it seemed to the French scouts who watched the glow of hundreds of camp fires in the darkness. However, the British had a surprise for the French. Late in the evening, the whole Anglo-American army was re-embarked, and by midnight, in strict silence, the fleet sailed past the French scouts undetected.

6 JULY: THE LANDING OF ABERCROMBY'S ARMY

By early light on 6 July, the leading bateaux were near the north end of Lake George at the "French Narrows" (Coate's Point and Black Point). Trépezec's detachment had been totally by-passed. However, a French canoe now came upon the British lead boats, quickly turned about and hurried back to shore. There were French advance posts in the area and, as the light became stronger, the small French detachments saw the multitude of bateaux before them. Resistance was out of the question and they rapidly retreated, carrying this latest news of the advance of Abercromby's army.

First ashore were parties of rangers, followed by American provincials, the light infantrymen of the 80th and the grenadiers from the six regular regiments who had been formed into a temporary shock battalion. They landed in the area now known as Howe's Landing. A hundred men of the 80th advanced, followed by the grenadiers, and found the area deserted. They were elated as resistance had been expected; instead, they found the outpost, a "strong entrenched camp" which had been set on fire and destroyed by the French who "retired very precipitately". The beach of the left bank and its immediate area was soon secured as more troops were landed. The beginning of a portage road on the right bank was also occupied by rangers, its entrenched camp also evacuated by the French. The whole army landed on the left bank without opposition; the only incidents reported being "a few popping Shots fired by the Enemy upon the Provincials who Landed on the right of the whole", according to Capt. Arnot of the 80th.

So far, everything was going wonderfully well for Abercromby and Howe. The Anglo-American army was now only 2 miles (4 km) from its objective. The French offered no resistance and seemed to be in retreat; they might even be trapped into Fort Carillon and would surely soon be vanquished by such a powerful army. Abercromby and Howe and their whole army must have felt that victory was within their grasp. In a matter of days, the fate of Canada might be sealed.

Sir William Johnson, superintendent of the Indian Department, arrived at Ticonderoga on the morning of 8 July with several hundred Mohawk Indians. He usually wore an all-scarlet coat with gold lace and buttons as shown in this miniature. (National Archives of Canada, C83497)

ENGAGEMENT AT BERNETZ BROOK, 6 JULY

ABERCROMBY'S ARMY MARCHES TOWARDS TICONDEROGA

By 10 am on the morning of 6 July, with the whole army safely ashore and the French seemingly on the run, an enthusiastic Lord Howe decided to press ahead immediately. His plan called for the army to march in columns to take possession of the west side of the La Chute River which connected Lake George to Ticonderoga. The river was unnavigable, with five rapids dropping by some 200 feet over a 2-mile stretch. With the British army coming this way, the French would not be able resist along the Portage Road, nor at the saw mills at the end of it, as their position would be turned. Thus, they would be trapped in the peninsula of Ticonderoga.

At two in the afternoon, the army was formed into three main columns. The left flank column was made up of American provincial troops mostly from Massachusetts. The center column had the 44th, 55th, 46th and 42nd regiments. The right column consisted of the 27th, the 4th and the six companies of the 1st battalions of the 60th. These three faced a difficult march through the woods.

A fourth column was headed by Lord Howe himself and mainly consisted of American provincial units: Putnam's Connecticut Rangers, Lyman's 1st Connecticut, Fitch's 3rd Connecticut, the New York and New Jersey regiments. A party of the 80th acted as forward skirmishers, following a trail edging the river. Rogers' Rangers had been sent ahead a couple of hours earlier to secure a stream the French called "Bernetz Brook" (now Trout Brook) so the whole army could cross it.

It was at this time that the good luck of the Anglo-Americans turned to bad. The trail near the river was clear and Howe sent the 1st and 3rd Connecticut regiments ahead to join Rogers at the brook. When they got there, Rogers was able to report that his scouts had found the French army camped only half a

Some 400 Mohawk warriors led by Sir William Johnson finally arrived at Ticonderoga on 8 July. They chose to sit out the contest and watched the battle from the slopes of Mount Defiance. (Print after Benjamin West)

CANADIAN INDIAN.

The fight at Bernetz Brook, on the afternoon of 6 July 1758, proved a tremendous loss to the British because of the death of Lord Howe, killed just as he arrived on the scene of the action. His dress and general appearance that day is conjectural but it should have been generally according to his own orders regarding the campaign dress of the troops. His hair was cut short, his hat would have had a narrow brim, his coats tails cut off and its lace removed. He is shown dressed in the colors of his own 55th Foot (scarlet faced with green, gold buttons) but there is no certainty in this. It was, however, almost certainly the dress of Capt. Monypenny, also of the 55th, who was near Lord Howe when he was killed. The troops with them mostly belonged to the 80th Light Armed Foot. A distinctive brown uniform was assigned to this light infantry unit.

P. Courcelle

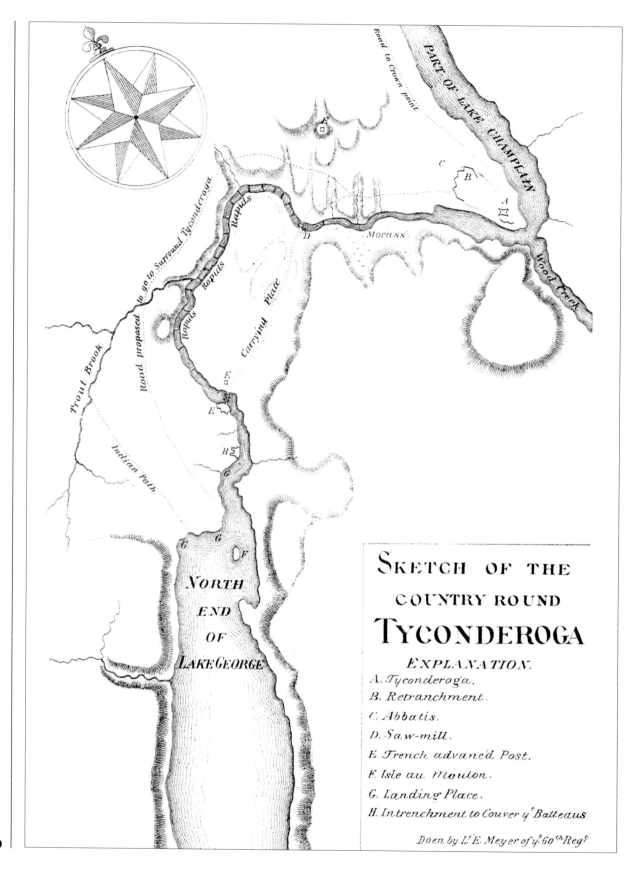

Road to Crown point

PART OF LAKE CHAMPLAIN

Wood Creek

Road proposed to go to Surround Tyconderoga

Rapids
Rapids
Rapids
Rapids
Rapids

Carrying Place

Morass

Trout Brook

Indian Path

E
E
H
G
G
G
F

D

NORTH
END
OF
LakeGeorge

SKETCH OF THE
COUNTRY ROUND
TYCONDEROGA
EXPLANATION.
A. Tyconderoga.
B. Retranchment.
C. Abbatis.
D. Saw-mill.
E. French advanc'd Post.
F. Isle au Mouton.
G. Landing Place.
H. Intrenchment to Couver y.e Batteaus.

Doen by L.t E. Meyer of y.e 60.th Reg.t

40

mile away at the saw mills. It was about four in the afternoon. What happened next, judging from the accounts of various participants and observers on both sides, was one of the more confused bush fights of the war.

Capt. Trépezec's 350-strong French scouting party lost its way in the forest when the Indian guides departed after seeing the Anglo-American armada. While they were trying to return to Ticonderoga, Abercromby's army had landed and actually by-passed them. On reaching Bernetz Brook, Trépezec's party was able to find its way and decided to follow the south bank of the brook to the La Chute River which would then take them to Fort Carillon and safety. Ensign Langy, who was heading the forward element of the French party, is said to have spotted something in the brush and shouted "Qui vive?" (Who goes there?) to which an English voice probably belonging to Lyman's 1st Connecticut Regiment responded, "Français," (the French), which did not fool Langy. "Feu! c'est l'ennemi," (Fire! It's the enemy), he immediately shouted to his men. They fired having no idea that the whole Anglo-American army was nearby. Rogers' Rangers with Lyman's and Fitch's regiments now turned on the French scouts and returned their fire. Some British accounts mentioned it was a French ambush, but it is clear from the French memoirs that it was an unexpected event. A fierce forest fight ensued.

When he heard the firing, Lord Howe immediately decided that his troops should counterattack and sweep off the French so as not to delay the march of the main body. He hurried to the scene of the action. What happened next was related by Capt. Alexander Monypenny, 55th Foot, Howe's brigade-major. He was near Lord Howe who "had just gained the top of a hill, where the firing was, when he was killed. Never ball had more deadly direction. It entered his breast on the left side, and (as the surgeons say) pierced his lungs, and heart, and shattered his backbone. I was about six yards from him, he fell on his back and never moved, only his hand quivered an instant."

The French were pushed back "fighting from tree to tree," Capt. Arnot noted; indeed, they were largely doomed and their route of withdrawal was by now mostly sealed up. Way over on the left column, Col. Bagley's Massachusetts Regiment had heard the firing and realized their unit was closest to the action. Eagerly Bagley's Regiment headed eastward until it engaged the rear of Trépezec's French scouting party, cutting off its retreat. Overwhelmed, the French fought on, losing about 150 men killed, wounded or drowned, while another 151 surrendered. Poularies later mentioned that many men in Trépezec's party had dampened their muskets in trying to cross Bernetz Brook which left them helpless. Hearing the musketry, Montcalm had rushed a few companies of grenadiers to the east bank of the La Chute River. Their fire stopped the pursuit by the Rangers and the New England troops, but only about 50 French soldiers managed to escape by swimming across the La Chute River, including Lt. Langy and a badly wounded Capt. Trépezec who died a few hours later. Another 50 escaped through the woods and made it to the French lines later.

The effect of this fiercely fought skirmish in the forest created profoundly disruptive commotion within the columns of the Anglo-American army. The sound of gunfire had produced considerable confusion in the various British columns struggling through the wood,

BRITISH FORCES
1 Lord Howe's column edging the La Chute River: Rangers, 80th Light Infantry, Lyman's 1st Connecticut Regiment, Fitch's 3rd Connecticut Regiment, New York Regiment and New Jersey Regiment
2 Rangers
3 Lyman's 1st Connecticut Regiment
4 Lord Howe with 80th Light Infantry, followed by the rest of his column
5 West Flank column: consists mostly of New England Provincial troops from Massachusetts
6 Bagley's Massachusetts Regiment

FRENCH FORCES
A Trépezec's Scouting Party: 250 detached from various French metropolitan regiments and about 100 colonial troops.

Phase 3 – **Early to mid afternoon: Captain Trépezec's French scouting party has become lost in the woods, but duting the early afternoon, it reaches the upper part of Bernetz Brook. Trépezec's party can now follow its south bank to the La Chute River and from there to Ticonderoga. They have no idea that the whole Anglo-American army is to their south.**

Phase 7 – **Late afternoon: Of the other Anglo-American columns, the most westerly, made up of New England provincials, makes the best progress. When firing is heard, Bagley's Massachusetts Regiment realizes it is closest to the action and heads towards the fight. In so doing, it arrives onto the flank and rear of Trépezec's French party, cutting off its retreat to the west. Already overwhelmed by the troops from Howe's column to the east, most of the French party is wiped out in forest fighting. However, the noise of the engagement at Bernetz Brook creates considerable confusion and fear in the two other Anglo-American columns. They take fright and turn towards the landing.**

Phase 6 – **About 1600–1630 hrs: Hearing the firing nearby to the north, Lord Howe hurries to the scene of the action taking the lead with a party of light infantry and the rest of his column following. As he arrives on the scene of the action, Lord Howe is instantly killed by a musket shot.**

ENGAGEMENT AT BERNETZ BROOK, 6 JULY 175

Phase 5 - **About 1600 hrs:** The forward elements of Trépezec's French party under Ensign Langy near the fork of Bernetz Brook. Suddenly they spot something in the brush. It is a detachment of the 1st Connecticut Regiment. The French fire immediately. A fierce and confused forest fight ensues.

Phase 2 – **Early to mid afternoon:** Major Robert Rogers and his rangers are sent ahead to scout the west bank along the La Chute River as scouts to reach and secure the fork of Bernetz Brook. Rogers remains at the fork and, finding no sign of the French army, sends rangers to scout further along the La Chute River. They spot French troops much further away, nearer to Fort Carillon, and report this back to Rogers.

BERNETZ BROOK

LA CHUTE RIVER

Phase 4 – **Mid afternoon:** As the trail near La Chute River is unhindered, Lord Howe detaches the 1st and 3rd Connecticut regiments ahead of his column to join and reinforce Rogers at the fork of Bernetz Brook. They reach Rogers at about 1530–1545 hrs and deploy to secure the area.

Phase 1 – **1400 hrs.** Four Anglo-American columns march into the woods heading north. The column edging the west bank of the La Chute River under Lord Howe makes the best progress thanks to a trail.

XX

HOWE

43

more or less lost. Many soldiers now thought it was Montcalm's army attacking them in the woods – and many must have remembered Braddock's disastrous defeat three years earlier in an equally alien environment at Monongahela. An officer of the 60th reported that some "soldiers were seized with panic, whole regiments fell back, and even the General [Abercromby] narrowly escaped being carried away in the crowd of fugitives."

The shocking news of Howe's death rapidly spread to the other corps; Abercromby was devastated to learn of the loss of his brilliant second-in-command. The skirmish had been really intense for about 20 minutes, but it had brought the advance of the Anglo-American columns to a halt; exactly the contrary to what should have been happening. It took hours to sort out the confusion, and as dusk fell, the uncertainty brought fears that the French and Indians were lurking nearby. The worst now happened as two columns mistook each other for the enemy and fired on each other through the wood. By the time the situation became clear, the columns were dispersed and Abercromby put a stop to everything for the night. As an officer of the 60th put it, the day had been "an extraordinary instance of 11,000 men being driven in and thrown into utter confusion by 350." The advance on Fort Carillon was totally ruined. The spirit of the army, so optimistic that morning, was now very gloomy and fearful; many men did not sleep that night. Anglo-American losses for the day are curiously not given, all the attention being devoted to Lord Howe, but might be estimated at about a hundred or so casualties between the fight and the incidents of "friendly fire" later on.

The death of Lord Howe was especially keenly felt in the Anglo-American camp. Almost every journal of the campaign noted the event with much gloom. Capt. Arnot mentioned the "unspeakable grief of the whole army", while Maj. William Eyre of the 44th reported that the event was "greatly lamented (and that with great justice) by the army." Something vital had been affected in the morale of the Anglo-American army. Several accounts noted that the spirit of the army seemed more sluggish afterwards. "This noble and brave officer being universally beloved by both officers and soldiers of the army, his fall was not only

The **Ticonderoga peninsula and Fort Carillon, as seen by lieutenants Clerk and Abercrombie and Capt. Stark and his rangers in the evening of 7 July 1758, must have looked almost similar to this view made by Capt. Thomas Davies over a year later. (National Archives of Canada, C10653)**

most sincerely lamented, but seemed to produce an almost general consternation and languor through the whole [army]," wrote Maj. Rogers. Thomas Mante, the contemporary British historian of the war, perhaps summed it up the best when he later wrote that, with Lord Howe's death, "the soul of the army seemed to expire."

7 JULY: BRADSTREET'S COLUMN SECURES THE PORTAGE ROAD

The dawn of 7 July found Abercromby's force spread all over the area in gloom and disorder. The regulars of the 44th and 55th regiments had returned to the landing place with some provincial units to regroup, probably the best thing to do under the circumstances. Abercromby called his officers to an early morning council of war to determine what to do next. There was little choice but to make the best of it, regroup and advance once again. After some tense discussions, Abercromby finally agreed to Bradstreet's proposal to march directly along the Portage Road to the saw mills, instead of trying to edge the La Chute River through the woods as on the previous day.

Bradstreet was entrusted with some 5,000 men, including the 44th Foot, six companies of the 1st Battalion of the 60th Foot, two Massachusetts provincial regiments, and two cannon with their gunners. Stark's company of rangers and some Stockbridge Indians would provide the advance parties. Bradstreet's column met no opposition, and by early afternoon was at the saw mills which had been mostly destroyed by the retreating French troops. Bradstreet sent word back to Abercromby that the burned-down saw mills had been occupied without any opposition and that the carpenters were already repairing the bridge which had been partly destroyed by the French. Obviously, after securing a good

Fort Carillon in c. 1757–58 according to a reconstruction of c. 1910. No evidence has since been found as to the existence of a tower (shown on the upper right) and the stylistic details of the buildings are open to interpretation. However, the general aspect with its bastions would have been generally as shown. (Print after Alfred Charles, Lord Bossom)

bridgehead on the north side of the La Chute River, Bradstreet was much tempted to push on ahead with his men, perhaps catch the French unprepared and proceed towards the fort. Abercromby ignored his request and instead ordered the remaining troops to join Bradstreet's column. During the late afternoon, Abercromby and the rest of the Anglo-American army arrived at the saw mills. They were eventually joined by another column made up of Rogers' Rangers, the 80th Light Infantry and Bagley's Massachusetts Regiment who arrived by trailing the west bank of the La Chute River.

One may wonder what might have happened if Bradstreet had been allowed to press ahead. In the best scenario Bradstreet might have come upon Montcalm's regiments still busy constructing their field fortifications and driven them into the fort. On the other hand, Montcalm had parties of lookouts watching the British. They had been instructed to warn him immediately of any suspicious moves so that the battalions could put down their axes, prime their muskets and man their entrenchments. Their field fortifications, it is true, would not have been as good in mid-afternoon as they were to be subsequently, but they were advanced enough in most places that the men had camouflaged part of them. Another consideration, no doubt much in the mind of Abercromby and some of his officers, was that there might be an ambush set up by the French and Canadians, the past masters at this type of warfare. At this point, the British had no intelligence of what was ahead so Gen. Abercromby's caution was certainly proper.

ABOVE LEFT **Private of a Massachusetts Provincial Regiment, 1758. The Massachusetts troops usually had coats of blue cloth with red facings at the time of the Ticonderoga campaign. Reconstitution by Herbert Knotel. (Anne S. K. Brown Military Collection, Brown University. Ph. R. Chartrand)**

ABOVE RIGHT **Officer, Grenadier Company, New Jersey Regiment, 1758. This was one of the only provincial regiments to have such a company. It was provided with 100 grenadier caps by the colony of New Jersey. Reconstitution by Herbert Knotel. (Anne S. K. Brown Military Collection, Brown University. Ph. R. Chartrand)**

IN THE FRENCH CAMP

MONTCALM JOINS HIS TROOPS

The first week of July had certainly been eventful for Abercromby's army. For Montcalm and his troops by comparison, it was a relatively quiet time when they were able to prepare for whatever might unfold. Montcalm followed his eight metropolitan army battalions to Fort Carillon, arriving on 30 June, and a week later, small detachments of colonial troops and militia were still trickling in.

Fusilier, La Reine Regiment, 1759. (Royal Library, Madrid)

Vaudreuil had chosen Montcalm's second-in-command, Brig. Gen. Lévis, to lead an attack on Albany itself, via Oswego and the Mohawk Valley using 400 colonial troops, 400 men detached from the army battalions and 800 militiamen. Naturally, Montcalm was totally opposed to any initiative taken by Vaudreuil, and this one was no different. In retrospect, it was not such a bad strategic idea; it might have split the Anglo-American forces and imposed a certain neutrality on the Iroquois in the colony of New York. If Lévis and his troops had left Canada earlier and threatened Albany while devastating the Mohawk Valley, Abercromby would have come under pressure from colonial officials and public opinion in New England – especially that of New York – to split or redirect his forces to face the threat. One part of his army might have tried to march on Fort Carillon, while another would have been deployed to protect the area menaced by Lévis' troops. However, none of that happened and, as July began, Abercromby and his formidable army stood on the shores of Lake George apparently unchallenged.

Montcalm certainly had a strong case when he felt he would need all the troops he could get at Ticonderoga. He had to stop what was obviously a major force assembling at the south of Lake George. On his arrival at Fort Carillon Montcalm was immediately briefed by the French scouts. The news they brought was pretty much what he expected. "The number of enemy troops," he wrote, "was growing daily" and they had an enormous amount of supplies. Only a few weeks previously, the site of Fort William-Henry had been a deserted and silent ruin; now the whole area was dotted with the tents, bustling with activity and the noise of what seemed to be an immense army. Anglo-American prisoners of war all had the same tale to tell their

French captors: their army was assembling, was very numerous and they were planning to attack Ticonderoga in early July. Since Abercromby's army was, according to Montcalm, only about 12 hours by boat from the north end of the lake, a landing at the head of the Portage Road could be expected and had to be countered. Montcalm believed that he was facing between 20,000 and 25,000 enemy troops.

Even before reaching Ticonderoga, Montcalm had already written ahead to Vaudreuil warning him that, from the intelligence received so far, a great army was assembling on the southern end of Lake George. To his credit, Vaudreuil took immediate action when he received this news. On 28 June, he canceled Levis' expedition and instructed him to go instead to Ticonderoga with the 400 metropolitan troops to reinforce Montcalm. Lévis left Montreal on 1 July.

At Ticonderoga itself, Montcalm's first move was to post his battalions. La Reine, Guyenne and Béarn under Bourlamarque went to build small makeshift redoubts to guard the head of the Portage Road at the northern end of Lake George. La Sarre, Royal-Roussillon, and Languedoc were posted to the west bank of the La Chute River with Montcalm. The second battalion of Berry was stationed in the area of the heights of Ticonderoga west of Fort Carillon; the third battalion was stationed in the fort itself. Two temporary companies of 100 men each were formed from volunteers from the eight metropolitan battalions. Capt. Bernard of the Béarn Regiment led one company, Capt. Duprat of La Sarre led the other. These volunteers were elite soldiers and acted as light infantry.

On 2 July, Montcalm went with Pontleroy, Desandrouin, Jacquot and Hébécourt, his specialist officers, to take stock of the land west of the fort and to "choose a field of battle and the position of an entrenched camp." His nervousness at facing such a powerful enemy was obvious. In his journal, he noted that time was short and that he lacked men, adding: "Our situation is critical. Activity and daring; these are our only resources." Looking around the area west of Fort Carillon, Montcalm and his officers decided to build the entrenched camp with *abbatis* on the heights of Ticonderoga. It would be the strongest position in a line that would start at the La Chute River to the south and run across the peninsula to the river leading north to Lake Champlain. The British would simply have to attack these heights as they would otherwise risk being outflanked if they ventured past either side. If they did, the fort's cannon had a clear field of fire. A second entrenchment line further back was also planned, its left being the fort and its right defended by a redoubt and an *abbatis* going to the river flowing north. In the event, there was little done on the second line as most efforts were to be devoted to the all-important entrenchments on Ticonderoga heights.

Count Maurès de Malartic (1730–1800), major of the Béarn Regiment posted at the right of the French *abbatis* during the battle, left fine memoirs of his campaigns in Canada. He later rose to general and colonial governor. This print shows him as an older man when he was governor-general of Ile-de-France (now Mauritius) and La Réunion between 1792 and 1800.

There was something almost desperate about the decision to build these lines. They really hemmed in the French defenders; but with the number of men available to Montcalm, there was not much choice. A French attack would have been suicidal against an enemy which he knew to be much stronger. Inevitably, the British would have to come out in the open and attack Ticonderoga. In an entrenched position on a height, the French army might stand a chance. However, should the battle be lost, it would be the end for Canada as most of its defenders would probably be killed, wounded, or taken prisoner. That was the gamble.

For Montcalm to succeed, two things were necessary: first, the Anglo-American force must be delayed, even if only for a day, so as to give his men more time to finish the entrenchments; second, Abercromby should decide to attack without waiting for his artillery to bombard the French positions. This second point was recognized by all in the French camp. Fort Carillon had been built to guard the narrow entrance to Lake Champlain as a forward post, albeit a strong one. It was not meant to sustain the assault of a large army equipped with siege artillery. The journals of several French officers mention that, if the enemy managed to install powerful batteries across the La Chute River on the slopes of the *Montagne des serpents à sonnette* (Rattlesnake Mountain, now called Mount Defiance), the fort's position would become most precarious. Therefore, the best defense rested on fortifying the heights west of the fort with lines of entrenched field works.

To plan all this was one thing but in order to build these lines, thousands of men would have to work very hard indeed for some days. As many troops were posted at the Portage Road, the work that could be done in the next few days would consist mostly of plotting the positions of the various field works. At this point, Montcalm needed the majority of his troops deployed in forward positions to wait for the British.

SCOUTING ABERCROMBY'S ARMY

Montcalm now needed all the information he could get about Abercromby's army at Fort William-Henry. Early on 4 July, Ensign de Langy

Jean-Guillaume de Plantavit, Comte de la Pause (1721–1804), was a captain in the Guyenne Regiment. He served in Canada from 1755 to 1760 and left a remarkably detailed journal. Back in France, he was knighted and promoted colonel in 1761. In 1776, he became a general and was made a count by Louis XVI. (Portrait of *c.* 1780 in a private collection)

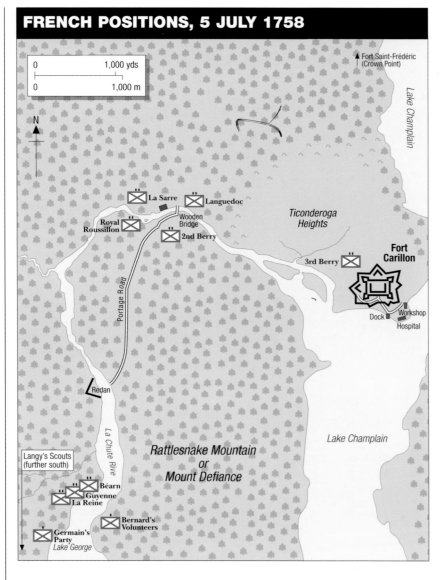

FRENCH POSITIONS, 5 JULY 1758

0   1,000 yds

0   1,000 m

N

Fort Saint-Frédéric
(Crown Point)

Lake Champlain

La Sarre

Languedoc

Royal
Roussillon

Wooden
Bridge

2nd Berry

Ticonderoga
Heights

3rd Berry

Fort
Carillon

Dock   Workshop

Hospital

Portage Road

Redan

La Chute River

Langy's Scouts
(further south)

Rattlesnake Mountain
or
Mount Defiance

Lake Champlain

Béarn

Guyenne

La Reine

Bernard's
Volunteers

Germain's
Party

Lake George

TOP RIGHT **Private, *Compagnies franches de la Marine*, the colonial regular infantry, c. 1757–60. A detachment of these troops usually provided the garrison in Fort Carillon and wore, as Mohawk scouts reported to Sir William Johnson in May 1757, "the common French uniform white & blew facings" in the fort. (Reconstruction by Eugène Lelièpvre, Parks Canada)**

BOTTOM RIGHT **Gun crew of the colonial artillery *canonniers-bombardiers* c. 1755–60. The dress worn and the type of gun served would have been much the same at Fort Carillon on 8 July 1758. (Reconstruction by Eugène Lelièpvre, Parks Canada)**

of the colonial troops was sent with 130 men to get as close as he could to Abercromby's camp and, if possible, kidnap some British soldiers for interrogation. Prisoners were not always dependable informants, but at least they gave some clues as to the strength and spirit of their army. Most crucial of all was an idea of the movements of the Anglo-American army. Langy was an excellent choice as he was an experienced scout who had spent part of his life in the wilderness. Two more parties under captains de Trépezec and Bernard were also sent south to watch the upper end of Lake George.

Generally, Indians were the best scouts on both sides. This time, however, they were not at Ticonderoga in large numbers, and were not part of the French scouting parties. The French-allied Indians were lukewarm supporters as they had been frustrated by the lack of booty in the previous campaigns and they sensed Montcalm's contempt for their practices, which is well documented in his journal and letters. They had recently heard and appreciated the soothing words and fine gifts of Governor-General Vaudreuil, but many remained hesitant. Their own

informants from New England were bringing word of unprecedented numbers of redcoats and American militiamen assembling. To this was added a certain reluctance, felt especially by the Canadian Iroquois allied to the French, to face in battle the New York Mohawk Iroquois, who were allied to the British, but nevertheless part of the same Indian nation.

On the morning of 5 July Langy's French scouts saw Abercromby's army moving north aboard "an innumerable number of barges" as the engineer Desandrouin observed. Langy rushed back to Ticonderoga and reported to Montcalm towards the evening of the same day. Montcalm now knew that the forward elements, followed by the whole Anglo-American army, were coming; he ordered the three battalions at the head of the Portage Road to withdraw to the lines near the fort and join the other regiments. The volunteer detachments were left behind to track the progress of the British. It was one of these units, under Capt. Germain, which greeted the British light infantrymen with musketry fire on the morning of the 6th before disappearing into the woods. Capt. Bernard's party also took pot-shots as it withdrew.

With about 100 men, Langy had gone back to join Capt. Trépezec's party on the west bank of upper Lake George. When it was time to return, they found that their Indian guides, overawed by the enormous

PLAN
du FORT
CARILLON
Echelle

British armada, had quietly disappeared. It was Trépezec's detachment
which became lost and ran into the British forces, killing Lord Howe.
But did the French know of their good fortune regarding Lord Howe?
Apparently not right away. Montcalm's and Bougainville's journals
mention his death, but obviously in hindsight as Bougainville stated that
Howe's body was buried in Albany. Other French accounts are in the
same vein or do not mention it. The best clue is perhaps from
Desandrouin, who wrote that several days after the main battle, British
officers told their French counterparts that the skirmish of the 6th had
been fatal to their hopes of success on the 8th.

Certainly, Montcalm and his men sensed something was strangely
wrong in the British camp, as their advance stopped and they

RIGHT **Ruins of one of Fort
Carillon's barrack buildings at
the end of the 19th century.**

entrenched themselves at the landings on both sides of the entrance of the La Chute River. The French expected them to rally and advance again on the 7th, so that the French field fortifications, already started on the 6th by the Berry Regiment, had to be made ready in all haste. Every battalion was put to work on building up the line on the heights as soon as the sun was up on the 7th; detachments of French scouts were posted to watch and warn of a sudden British advance. They reported regularly to Montcalm of the progress of Bradstreet's men who were cautiously advancing up the Portage Road to the saw mills. Capt. de la Pause noted in his journal that "all day, our volunteers exchanged shots with the enemy light infantry." Still by day's end, he further noted that Abercromby with "a great part of his militias and the rest of his regular troops had advanced up to the La Chute" River at the saw mills. Several boats and pontoons had been seen crossing, "mounted with two pieces of cannons" landing troops on the north side of the river. The Anglo-American units were now very cautious, "each building several entrenchments one after the other" as they advanced closer to the French army's position on the heights.

THE LINE OF ENTRENCHMENTS

On the heights of Ticonderoga, the eight French metropolitan battalions worked with considerable energy during 7 July to erect as much of the

abbatis as they could. Everyone knew that the chances of success against the forthcoming British attack depended on the construction of those earthworks. Montcalm noted that even the regimental officers could be seen "ax in hand, giving the example" to their men. The engineer Desandrouin was less impressed by the regimental officers he saw, the majority of whom, in his view, showed incredible "indolence" and lack of attention to the work. In any event, the men, with at least some officers, worked very hard. Each battalion planted its colors in the area it was working which must have been a source of pride as they toiled. The urgency of the matter was certainly felt by all, and they worked "with such an incredible ardor", Montcalm reported, that, by early evening, the line was in a good state of defense. However, many French soldiers continued to work into the night as the Anglo-Americans camped nearby could testify from all the noise they made.

Montcalm described the works built by his men on 7 July as follows:

"The left rested on a steep slope eighty toises [156 meters] from the La Chute River, the summit crowned with *abbatis*. This *abbatis* flanked a gap between which we were going to place six cannon to cover it as well as the river. The right also rested on a height whose slope was not so steep as that on the left. The plain, between this height and the St Frédéric River, was flanked by a branch of our entrenchments on the right, and should have been covered by a battery of four guns which was finished after the battle of the eight [of July]. Moreover, the cannon of

Traces of the French entrenchment lines to the northwest visible today. The terrain, which is now a forest, drops sharply just beyond the trees. (Photo: RC)

Some of the remains of the entrenchments to the west as seen today. There was a clear field of fire in 1758, but trees have since grown all over the area. (Photo: RC)

the fort were pointed towards this plain as well as towards the landing place they [the enemy] could use on our left. The center followed the contours of the land, always keeping to the high ground of the heights, and all parts of it flanking each other. Several places, in truth, as well as on the right, were subject to enemy cross fire; but this was because we did not have enough time to put up traverses. These sorts of entrenchments were made of tree trunks, lying one on top of the other, and having felled trees before them whose branches were cut and made pointed giving the effects of *chevaux-de-frise*."

La Pause also described these works in detail, as well as several long orders regarding the measures to be taken for their defense, all of which take several pages of his papers. Each battalion was to be provided with a depot of 200 lbs of powder and 400 lbs of balls, in addition to the cartridges already issued; each man was to keep 15 in reserve, with an extra flint. To shoot faster, only powder and ball would be used when the enemy was at close range. Dry leaves could be used to prevent the balls from rolling out of the barrel if pointing downwards. A reserve of 50 extra muskets was also issued to each battalion. Soldiers were to bring their axes to use against any enemy soldiers who scaled the entrenchment walls in case space was too restricted to fix bayonets. Stones were to be kept handy to throw down on the attackers, as well as a few grenades primed with wicks. A "depot" (a small powder magazine) was built and covered for protection behind the colors of each battalion's sector to house ammunition which was handed out by a sergeant who kept a record of issues. A general reserve depot was also built in the center of the French position to supply the battalions with extra powder and ball barrels. Each battalion had one or two covered barrels of water to put out fires, and further barrels of fresh drinking water were behind the line. Designated soldiers were to bring pails of drinking water up to the men during the action.

The entrenchments were far from perfect, as Montcalm had noted about the traverses. Desandrouin, who was directing the works and seemed to be everywhere at the same time, was especially critical, perhaps because he was a trained engineer, and could see that they were not always built "by the book." According to his account, many also lacked firing steps because they were built too low. There had been no time to build the artillery batteries on either side and install the guns. On the other hand, there could be no doubt that an extraordinary feat had been accomplished in a single day. By the evening of 7 July, the entrenched position on the heights, with its protective *abbatis* in front, was built up and just about ready.

Reasonably secure, the French were further encouraged on the evening of the 7th by the arrival of Gen. Lévis, Montcalm's popular second-in-command. Lévis' 400 men, who had been detached from the metropolitan battalions, provided a much needed reinforcement of regular troops just in the nick of time, and were greeted with considerable joy in the camp, Montcalm noted. It was a great morale boost.

Remains of a trench to the west, overgrown with trees. (Photo: RC)

BATTLE AT TICONDEROGA, 8 JULY 1758

OBSERVATIONS OF THE FRENCH LINES

Lt. Clerk, the senior engineer, and his assistant Capt. James Abercrombie of the 42nd Foot, one of Gen. Abercromby's ADCs, were at the saw mills, and wanted to see Fort Carillon and the French lines. Clerk was also keen to find sites where an artillery battery could be sited that might enfilade an exposed part of the entrenchments. So, in the late afternoon of 7 July, with Capt. Stark and an escort of rangers, they went off to climb Rattlesnake Mountain to have a good view of Fort Carillon. Once they got high up, the view was superb. Not only could they see the fort clearly, but also thousands of French soldiers digging trenches and field fortifications about a kilometer to the west of the fort. It seemed to them that these works were relatively simple and unimpressive. From what they could see, much work still needed to be done by the French troops before these defenses could become truly formidable.

What they could not know, observing from a distance of about two kilometers, was that much of the sturdy earthwork and log walls were in fact already built. The main entrenchments and *abbatis* were just about

The battle of Ticonderoga, 8 July 1758, as seen by this widely distributed mid-19th-century engraving. It is a spirited illustration of the Anglo-American attack, but full of anachronisms, such as cannon on the French *abbatis*, horses and colors for the attacking British. (National Archives of Canada, C4664)

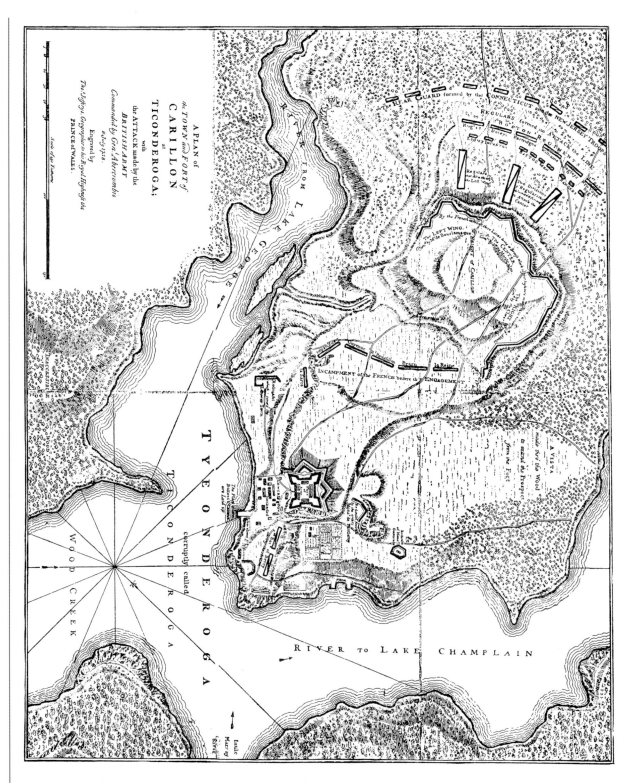

Plan of Fort Carillon and the attack on Ticonderoga, 8 July 1758, by Thomas Jefferys. This plan is the best-known and most widely published of the various maps of the battle. It is said to have been based on the map made by Lobtinière which was found in Quebec City following its capture the following year, but the trench line north and south of the height has been left out, and the island in the La Chute River is smaller.

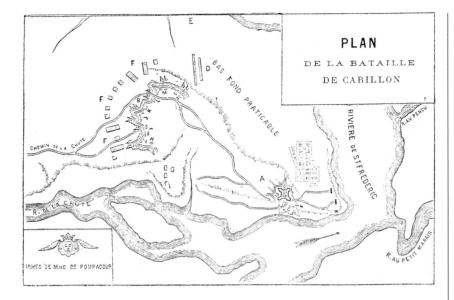

Plan de la bataille de Carillon after an original which bore the seal of Madame de Pompadour. A: Fort Carillon. B: *abbatis*. C: lower town and landing below the fort. D: colonial troops and Canadian militiamen. E: clear field. F: British columns. G: volunteers of Bernard and Duprat. H: La Sarre. I: Languedoc. J: Berry. K: Royal-Roussillon. L: Guyenne. M: Béarn. N: La Reine. (From H. R. Casgrain, Les Français au Canada, Tours, 1926)

finished and had been camouflaged by fir trees and shrubs to fool observers; the French fully expected that enemy scouts would be watching from a distance on a nearby mountain. As it turned out, their camouflage stratagem was destined to work far better than any of them would have dared to hope. The young British officers believed that the French field works were unfinished and relatively negligible. This is what they reported when they went back down to the saw mills. Gen. Abercromby and his staff were heartened to learn this; a daring action would restore the army's spirit dampened by Lord Howe's death, and might overcome the French before they were ready, perhaps concluding the campaign with few casualties. Still, the moment called for some caution. It was wise to plan for at least an artillery battery on the south side of the La Chute River so guns were ordered up. Most of all, another scout to confirm what had been seen by the young engineers was required.

Early on 8 July, Bradstreet and a "foreign engineer" went out and cautiously approached the heights. The foreign engineer was probably Lt. Charles Rivez, 60th Foot, a French Huguenot officer with engineering experience. They came upon a field work, undetected, and examined it from a safe distance. It was indeed not a very formidable affair. Otherwise the field seemed clear and if there were elaborate entrenchments, they were much further back and within the range of the fort's cannon, concluded Rivez. They went back to their own camp to join a council of war called by Abercromby to plan the day ahead.

The senior regular officers (the provincial officers were not invited) assembled at that momentous council now had Clerk's report and its confirmation by Bradstreet and Rivez. They also had a plan of the grounds and the entrenchments to examine, submitted by Clerk from his observations of the previous afternoon. In his later report to William Pitt, Abercromby stated that "on the morning of the 8th, I sent Mr. Clerk, across the river, on the opposite side of the fort, in order to reconnoiter the enemy's position. Upon his return, and a favorable report of the practicability of carrying these works, if attacked before they were finished, it was agreed to storm them that very day." Indeed, his letter to

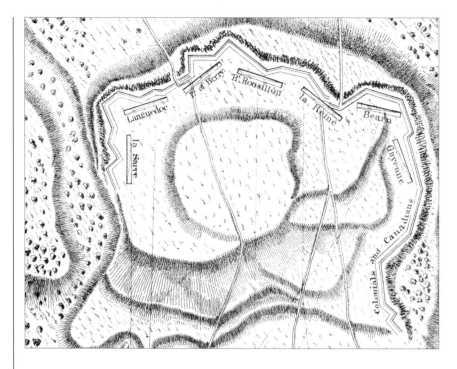

Pitt would make it seem that Clerk was present in person at the council. Instead, he had indeed been sent on a morning scout to the south side of the La Chute River, primarily to choose a site for a battery at the foot of Rattlesnake Mountain. Perhaps he even had time to return, reporting to Abercromby that the French positions still seemed harmless, before arranging to move the guns up. In the event, those present at the council had his map and report which were now confirmed by Bradstreet and Rivez's scout. Reports, from deserters and prisoners, encouraged Abercromby to believe that Montcalm had about 6,000 men at Ticonderoga and that another 3,000 Canadians with Indians were on their way to join him. By striking now, that junction could be avoided. Victory seemed ensured as the French were obviously unprepared and their works could easily be stormed.

One may wonder, in light of subsequent events, on what premiss the decision to attack was based. Which, in turn, begs the question: what did the scouts really see? Clerk, Abercrombie and Stark had seen the French works from far away on top of Rattlesnake Mountain, not perceiving that more earthworks were covered by camouflage. Bradstreet and Rivez had seen the entrenchments too – or had they? About 50 meters in front of their *abbatis* which lay ahead of the main entrenchment on the heights, Montcalm had posted a string of French detachments to warn his army in the event of any surprise attack. Just in front of these detachments was a very simple, vaguely fence-like log line which was really the outer line of the *abbatis* and not the main works. Situated on rising ground, these could be taken for simple field works; it must have been what Bradstreet and Rivez saw and assumed to be the main entrenchments. To see the real line of entrenchments, they would have had to cross this first obstacle; but then they would have run into the soldiers of the French detachments. Indeed, they probably saw some of them as they sneaked up to reconnoiter the position, convinced that this was the main works.

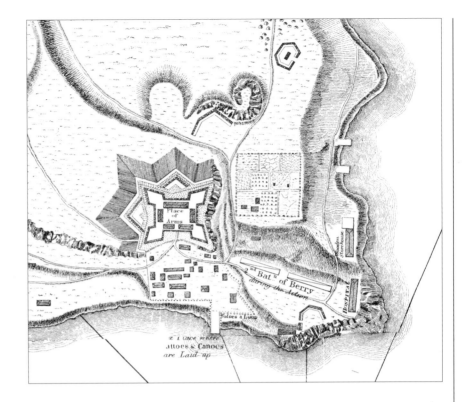

MOVING IN FOR THE ATTACK

Since the death of Lord Howe, Gen. Abercromby was in something of a vacuum regarding tactical advice. The post of second-in-command devolved by seniority to Brig. Gen. Thomas Gage, but in these crucial days, he was almost invisible. His whereabouts are still largely undocumented. The reasons for this are equally unclear, but one factor is evident: his influence was negligible. It was Lt. Col. Bradstreet, the keen and daring colonial officer, who seems to have had much of Abercromby's attention. Abercromby was anxious to move as soon as possible. So was Bradstreet. Clerk's survey, now confirmed by Bradstreet's and Rivez's dawn scout, left few doubts. The weak French field works were to be attacked now before they were reinforced.

"Accordingly," Abercromby later wrote, "the Light Infantry, and the Right Wing of the Provincials were ordered immediately to March, and post themselves, out of cannon shot of the entrenchment, their right extending to Lake George [meaning the La Chute River], & their left to Lake Champlain, in order that the [British] regular troops, destined for the attack of the entrenchments might form in their rear."

The 80th Light Infantry, the rangers, the battoemen and the provincial units formed themselves into a skirmish line which actually could only cover the main French entrenchments on the heights. The position of the units in this forward line was approximately as follows: on the right (or south) was the light infantry; at the center were the battoemen; on the left (or north) were the rangers. Behind the rangers was the first battalion of the New York Regiment. Behind the battoemen and light infantry were first Bagley's, then Williams', Partridge's, Doty's,

61

Ruggle's and Preble's Massachusetts regiments. This sequence, based on Capt. Dubois' account, agrees with Thomas Jefferys' plan of the attack, except that the line ends at Ruggle's. Preble's Massachusetts Regiment is not mentioned by Jefferys, but it was certainly there as it suffered casualties.

Behind the New York and Massachusetts provincials, the British regiments then came into position, formed three deep, divided into their usual three brigades :

Left Brigade: *c.* 2,100 men under Lt. Col. William Haviland, 27th Foot – Blakeney's 27th Foot; the six companies of the 1st Bn., 60th Foot; 4th Bn., 60th Foot.

Center Brigade: *c.* 1,500 men under Lt. Col. John Donaldson, 55th Foot, – Abercromby's 44th Foot and Lord Howe's 55th.

Right Brigade: *c.* 1,600 men under Lt. Col. Francis Grant, 42nd Foot – 42nd and 46th regiments.

The six grenadier companies, about 600 strong, were brigaded together into a temporary unit under Lt. Col. Frederick Haldiman, 60th Foot.

Finally, behind the British regulars was the rearguard formed by the Connecticut and New Jersey provincial regiments.

Abercromby's plan was a sound one for a classic frontal assault. Skirmishers would go in first, followed by the provincials who would test the defenses; the regular columns would then come up simultaneously to storm and take the defenses. This had good chances of success provided the formation held, the attack was coordinated, and the objective clearly known.

Montcalm and his officers and men had taken various measures to have advance warning of a British attack. Most of the army was sleeping in a tent camp set up between the entrenchments on the heights and the fort. Each battalion and the colonial troops provided 75-man detachments which stayed on the heights, some sleeping, some

BELOW LEFT **Regimental color of the Royal-Roussillon Regiment. The quarters were blue, red, brown and green with gold lilies on the cross. Each battalion of French line infantry had two colors. Royal regiments generally had gold lilies ornamenting the cross. (Anne S. K. Brown Military Collection, Brown University. Ph. R. Chartrand)**

BELOW CENTER **Regimental color of the La Reine Regiment. The quarters were green and black. This was the queen's regiment which was denoted by the ornamented cross with crowns and *fleurs de lys*. (Anne S. K. Brown Military Collection, Brown University. Ph. R. Chartrand)**

BELOW RIGHT **Regimental color of the La Sarre Regiment. The quarters were red and black. (Anne S. K. Brown Military Collection, Brown University. Ph. R. Chartrand)**

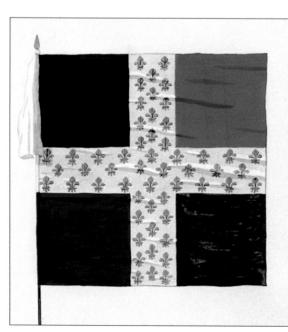

on guard along the entrenchment walls. Outside the entrenchments, about 50 meters in front of the field of *abbatis*, was another string of detached soldiers: the south, or French left, had fusiliers from metropolitan regiments; the center had grenadiers; the right had 75 colonial infantrymen. They were to watch for enemy noise and movement, and skirmish with the enemy advance parties to slow them down while retreating to the main lines.

"Long before dawn" on 8 July, Malartic recalled, the French drummers beat "*La Généralle*" which roused the army and soon the troops and their officers were taking up positions on the heights of Ticonderoga. The army was disposed as follows:

> South (or French left) flank: La Reine Brigade, *c.* 886 men commanded by Col. Bourlamarque – battalions of La Sarre (460 men) and Languedoc (426 men).
>
> Center: Royal-Roussillon Brigade, *c.* 930 men under the direct command of Gen. Montcalm – 2nd Berry (480 men) and Royal-Roussillon (450 men) battalions.
>
> Northeast (or French right): La Reine Brigade, *c.* 1,225 men led by Gen. Lévis – La Reine (345 men), Béarn (410 men) and Guyenne (470 men) battalions.

Covering the entrenchments to the north were about 450 colonial troops and Canadian militiamen. The volunteer companies of Duprat and Bernard covered the southern side. In Fort Carillon were about 400 men of the third battalion of Berry with 50–60 colonial artillerymen.

Once the battalions had planted their colors in their respective areas and taken up their positions, they continued raising the height of the walls of the entrenchments and building up an earthen embankment on the French left (or southern) flank which might afford some protection should the British install a battery on Rattlesnake Mountain across the La Chute River. A battery and a redoubt were also being erected to better secure this area, but it still needed a great deal of work before

guns could be installed. Work continued on the French right (or northern) flank from the main entrenchments on the height to Lake Champlain, a distance of some 350 meters, but the 450 colonial infantrymen and Canadian militiamen could not erect anything like finished field fortifications over such a distance. A battery was supposed to flank it at its northern end near Lake Champlain, but construction had hardly started and it certainly had no guns. Some maps show nothing in this area, while others have an outline of the works to be done. On the morning of 8 July, there must have been little beyond a fence or trench line. This was the weakest point in the French position. Its one advantage was that there were few trees between this line and Fort Carillon so it offered a clear field of fire for the fort's artillery, should a British force attempt to overcome it.

With his troops now in position on the heights in the entrenchments, Montcalm ordered that each battalion's grenadier company and a piquet would stand as a reserve with fixed bayonets behind its own battalion, ready to help at any spot where the enemy breached the fortifications. The 50-man grenadier company of 3rd Berry was joined to the seven others although the rest of the battalion was in the fort. The fusiliers at the wall were selected, as far as possible, from the best shots of their companies. They were to always make aimed shots at close range, and used loaded muskets passed on by their comrades. Thus, instead of the usual two or three unaimed shots a minute, some six to eight aimed shots a minute were possible.

During the middle of the morning, the French noticed a lot of movement on the flank of Rattlesnake Mountain. They quickly saw these were not British or New England troops, but Indians making much noise with their hostile war cries and shooting. Some 400, mostly Mohawk, warriors had just arrived with Sir William Johnson and were "painted all sorts of colors" according to Massachusetts soldier Amos Richardson. Although they were out of musket range, they made a considerable show of themselves with a great deal of shooting which, Montcalm, La Pause and other French officers related, "did not interrupt our work" and to which the French soldiers did not even respond. After a while, Sir William's Indians settled down. European-style linear warfare and all-out assaults on fortified positions were completely unlike their way of war. They decided to watch the oncoming battle sitting on the flanks of a mountain which offered them a first-class view.

THE FIRST ATTACK GOES WRONG

Around 10 am, the Anglo-American forward line of light infantry, battoemen and rangers started moving out cautiously. They were followed by the line of New York and Massachusetts provincial regiments. The lead unit was Capt. Stark's company of rangers, followed closely by Maj. Rogers and the rest of the rangers. To their right, somewhat behind them, were the battoemen, and further right were Gage's 80th Light Infantrymen.

First contact, predictably, was made by rangers of Stark's company. Rogers recorded that at about 300 yards from the breastworks "my advance guard was ambushed and fired upon by 200 Frenchmen". It was not actually an ambush, but a much smaller party of the French sentries posted in front of the *abbatis* to warn of the oncoming advance of the Anglo-Americans. This was somewhat to the right of the rangers' position. However, hearing this, Rogers "immediately formed a front" with the men he was leading and marched up to assist Stark's advance guard who had "maintained their ground". When the French soldiers saw more rangers coming, they "immediately retreated" according to Rogers.

Shortly thereafter, at about 12.30 pm, de Lancey's New York Regiment had formed on the extreme left and were advancing. Because Rogers' rangers had veered somewhat to the right, they were not protected by the skirmish line which was supposed to be in front of them. Sure enough, they too came under fire from the French forward piquets as they got closer to the *abbatis* line while believing that they were "in the rear of our friends" (the rangers). Instead, they were "surprised by the enemy, about 300 yards from the breast-works who fired upon us," reported Capt. Dubois. The New Yorkers reacted swiftly, formed up, fired back and, with a "huzza" cheer, charged the French who "were repulsed and driven by the heat of our people into their trenches."

These first contacts were most encouraging, with the French already on the run and part of their entrenchments breached, or so it seemed to the rangers and the New Yorkers. The shooting on the left drew the attention of Lt. Col. Haviland who was coming up from behind with his brigade consisting of the 27th and the 60th. Haldiman's grenadier brigade was also nearby, as was a body of detached regular piquets under Maj. Proby of the 55th. At this point, Haviland made a momentous decision which was to profoundly influence the subsequent events: he decided that his regular brigade should advance and attack the French. He therefore instructed Rogers to provide cover with his rangers until his regulars had by-passed them and assaulted the French. From what he was told of the New Yorkers' and the rangers' attacks, Haviland believed that they had penetrated the French entrenchments and hurried to provide support. Formed into columns, Haviland's brigade, with Proby's men in the vanguard, charged ahead.

Curiously, as the British brigade surged forward, they found that the French had vanished, and instead Haviland's men were charging into a hidden *abbatis* (an obstacle made up of logs with sharpened branches). As the soldiers struggled over and around the obstacles, sometimes ending up in single file, their formation disintegrated. "Unhappy for us," Maj. Eyre later wrote, "we presently found it a most formidable entrenchment and not to be forced by the method we were upon. For upwards of one hundred yards in front of it, trees were fell down in such manner that it broke our battalions before we got near the breastworks, as we marched a battalion in front three deep." They were now being

Montcalm at Carillon from an illustration in a 1915 *Histoire du Canada* school book read by generations of young Quebec children. There were no cannon installed in the French *abbatis* lines on 8 July, although some were added during the following days.

BATTLE OF TICONDEROGA, 8 JULY 1758 1000–1300 HRS

Phase 1 – 1000 hrs: Both armies are in position. The main body of French troops, consisting of seven battalions, is deployed behind the log wall on the heights of Ticonderoga. The British are formed into four lines: in front, a line of skirmishers consisting of rangers, battoemen and light infantry; the New York and Massachusetts provincial regiments follow; then the three brigades of British regulars and Haldiman's grenadiers; as a rear guard the New Jersey and Connecticut regiments. Coming out of the woods, the forward elements cautiously advance towards the French position.

LA CHUTE RIVER

TICONDEROGA HEIGHTS

ANGLO-AMERICAN UNITS

1 Rangers
2 Corps of Armed Battoemen
3 80th Light Infantry
4 New York Regiment
5 Massachusetts provincial regiments: Bagley's, William's, Partridge's, Doty's, Ruggle's, Preble's
6 Haviland's Left Brigade: 27th, 1/60th (6 cos.), 4/60th
7 Haldiman's Grenadiers
8 Donaldson's Centre Brigade
9 Grant's Right Brigade: 42nd, 44th
10 New Jersey provincial regiment
11 Connecticut and Rhode Island provincial regiments
12 Mohawk Indians

FRENCH UNITS

A La Sarre (Bourlamarque's La Sarre Brigade)
B Languedoc (Bourlamarque's La Sarre Brigade)
C 2/Berry (Montcalm's Royal-Roussillon Brigade)
D Royal-Roussillon (Montcalm's Royal-Roussillon Brigade)
E La Reine (Lévis' La Reine Brigade)
F Béarn (Lévis' La Reine Brigade)
G Guyenne (Lévis' La Reine Brigade)
H *Compagnies franches de la Marine* and Canadian Militia
I Duprat's and Bernard's volunteer companies
J 3/Berry
K *Canonniers-Bombardiers* attending batteries in Fort Carillon

XXX

ABERCROMBY

Phase 4 – **About 1300 hrs:** Hearing the New Yorkers cheer, Haviland decides on his own to commit his brigade to give them support and consolidate their success by charging in. Haldiman's grenadiers follow suit. To their surprise, instead of the main French position, they now discover themselves struggling into *abbatis* camouflaged by greenery and come under heavy fire from the French main position at the log wall. By now Gen. Abercromby has totally lost control of his troops.

Phase 2 – **About 1200–1230 hrs:** the Rangers run into the French forward pickets. Rather than providing cover on the left, they veer to the right in pursuit of the French.

4

F

G

H   H

FORT CARILLON

K

J

LAKE CHAMPLAIN

N

Phase 3 – **About 1230–1300 hrs:** The New York Provincial Regiment on the left has now no skirmishers to cover its advance. It also runs into French forward pickets on the edge of the *abbatis*. Mistaking the *abbatis*' edge for the main French entrenchment of log walls, it charges with a 'huzaa' thinking they are capturing part of the main works. In fact, the French forward pickets are ordered to withdraw into the main position, beyond the *abbatis*.

XX

MONTCALM

fired upon quite heavily from beyond the *abbatis*, Eyre being one of the wounded. The British at last realized the true position of the French entrenchment; what the rangers and New Yorkers had seen and taken were merely parts of the fence-like line in front of the *abbatis* held by Montcalm's advance parties. Haviland's men tried to push on, but the odds were too heavy and, with losses mounting rapidly, they retreated to regroup.

Haldiman's grenadiers also advanced, but tangled in branches and under heavy fire, they too suffered heavily. Lt. William Grant, of the 42nd's grenadier company, recalled that the *abbatis* had completely upset the grenadiers' ranks, "making it impossible for us to keep our order", while being mowed down "like a field of corn" by the French "wall pieces and small arms" before the grenadiers could "fire a single shot". Soon, Grant himself had his "fuzee broke" in his hand and then suffered a "shot through the middle of the groin," but was fortunately taken away by a couple of his grenadiers to a makeshift shelter hastily built up by soldiers of Ruggle's Massachusetts Regiment just beyond the *abbatis*. With his column practically destroyed, and recognizing that an assault on the French entrenchments was almost impossible, Haldiman ordered the remaining grenadiers to retreat.

Probably no one was more puzzled and upset than Gen. Abercromby at this point. With his ADC, Capt. Abercrombie, the general went up with the 42nd to the line of *abbatis*. He first believed that only the rangers and provincials had been engaged, "but to his great surprise" found that the regulars were also attacking the French position. He had given no orders for the assault. Instead of the coordinated attack he had planned, there was now a premature, unplanned and unmanageable affair already engrossing the left of his army. The ADC later recollected that it was Gen. Abercromby's positive wish for "the Attack not to begin till the whole Army was formed" in battle order, and that such a command was only then to be given. Instead, the attack had begun in one place, was being repulsed and all was confusion. Once again, as on 6 July, the command discipline of the army fell short in spite of the general's orders to observe stricter discipline. Whatever control he had over the army was now gone and almost impossible to regain.

With coordination now lost, the British attack entered a phase described by Maj. Eyre as being "left for each commanding officer" to attack and support when he could. At the edge of the *abbatis*, Haviland's and Haldiman's survivors were regrouping; assorted rangers, battoemen and light infantrymen of the 80th were now returning fire using the *abbatis* logs as cover, and their well-aimed shots probably caused the first casualties in the French entrenchments.

Meanwhile the 44th and 55th regiments on the edge of the *abbatis* were getting ready to go in; the 46th and the 42nd were hurrying to get into position towards the British left as this seemed to be where the attack was being pursued. With a brigade going from right to left, Abercromby's order of attack was now totally muddled, but curiously, he does not seem to have attempted to correct the situation. Things had gone wrong from the start of the advance and it would appear that, considering the difficulties of communications on a battlefield, everything was left to area commanders. They, in turn, could do little besides trying to overcome the French lines by the sheer courage and determination of their men.

Montcalm at Carillon in a 1940s picture by the Canadian historical illustrator C. W. Jefferys, possibly the best-known image of the battle by English Canadians. The uniforms and arms of the French soldiers are inaccurate in various details (for instance the officers did not have pikes and the uniforms no lapels) but it gives a fair idea of what the French line might have looked like.

Abercromby appears to have had no alternate plans such as trying to outflank the French entrenchments, or to retreat and wait for the artillery. He thus seems to have been overcome by events, a serious fault for a commander-in-chief. Still, one cannot help but to wonder where his second-in-command, Gen. Gage, was. If anyone might have brought up new ideas to deal with the difficult obstacle put up by Montcalm, it should have been Gage as he had novel tactical concepts. Amazingly, there is no trace of him in contemporary memoirs and his papers are equally uninformative as to his whereabouts on 8 July as in previous days. Of course, ultimate responsibility must rest with Abercromby, but he was certainly left to himself by Gage. As for Bradstreet, who had filled in the previous day as an unofficial second-in-command, he was back in the line with his battoemen. The British senior command was thus most deficient for the task ahead.

IN THE FRENCH LINES

The situation was very different behind the French entrenchment walls. Every man was in his designated spot, with the best shots at the loopholes, their officers posted intermittently along the parapet, grenadiers and piquets behind. The battalion commanders were in the vicinity of the colors and the brigade commanders would have moved around their respective sector.

They had ample warning from the brush with the rangers and the New Yorkers at the outer edge of the *abbatis*. Their forward parties had given several volleys as much to give warning to the French line as to slow down the Anglo-American skirmishers. They then retreated in orderly fashion inside the main entrenchment, as planned, while their last skirmishers kept taking odd shots at the oncoming Anglo-Americans. The accounts of Montcalm and several other observers reported gladly that none of the soldiers of the forward parties had been lost in the early skirmishes. Lévis observed that, in general, the four British columns first coming on the field of battle did not seem to have any specific target other than "the right, the left and the center," and that the column to the French right first veered towards the center column which, in turn, made the center column lean towards the French left where he commanded and where two columns now attacked. The engagement became most intense. Lévis ordered La Reine to move closer to Guyenne so they could double-up as he felt, rightly, that the enemy was going "to make a considerable effort" to attack the French right. The two British columns, which would have been Haviland's with Haldiman's grenadiers, did attack and, according to Lévis, tried to outflank the entrenchment. As they struggled through the *abbatis*, the British regulars came within easy range of Lévis' sector and were repulsed by the Béarn, Guyenne and La Reine regiments.

"At the start of the affair," wrote Bougainville, who probably meant during the first attack on the French right, something of a panic set in when "a large number" of uncertain and frightened Canadian militiamen posted north of the entrenchments panicked and fled "towards the boats". In Fort Carillon, the colonial gunners spotted their movement and opened up artillery fire to stop them. "One of these fugitives was wounded" and this sobering reminder convinced them to run back to their trenches. However, there was no way they would come out again from their hiding places but, concluded Bougainville, "these were not Canadians of the good sort." The regular colonial troops posted there held their positions.

The British column at the other end of the battlefield, consisting of the 42nd and 44th, now attacked the French left and finding it almost impassable, veered further left in an attempt to outflank the heights. The volunteer companies of Duprat and Bernard, with grenadiers and piquets of Royal-Roussillon, stopped the British column which, according to Desandrouin, allowed the battalions of La Sarre and Guyenne in the entrenchments on the heights to launch a withering fire forcing the British to retreat. Yet another column, made up of the 46th and the 55th, attacked the center hoping to penetrate through a gully, but it was driven back by Berry, while another column was beaten

ABOVE LEFT **Soldier with color, Béarn Regiment, c. 1757–60. The quarters were buff or light brown with two red horizontal center bars. (Parks Canada)**

ABOVE CENTER **Soldier with color, Guyenne Regiment, c. 1757–60. The quarters were light brown and green. (Parks Canada)**

ABOVE RIGHT **Soldier with color, Languedoc Regiment. The quarters were buff or light brown and violet. The regiment changed uniforms in 1761 and again in 1763 when the green collar and lapels shown were adopted. (Parks Canada)**

back by Royal-Roussillon further towards the French right. It was about 2 pm or sometime thereafter, and all the British assaults were failing

BRITISH BARGES REPULSED

At about this time the French spotted on their left about 20 barges full of men, as well as two large rafts with cannon on the La Chute River which had a large, flat and marshy island at its mouth, edging the north shore. The heavily laden barges were approaching the north shore and were met by brisk musketry fire from Bernard's and Duprat's two volunteer companies which had been posted between the entrenchments and the river. However, the barges continued on. In Fort Carillon the colonial gunners, the *canonniers-bombardiers*, had seen the barges too, and trained their guns on them. The big guns in the southwest bastion opened fire and sank one barge; more shots were fired and another barge was hit and broken apart. At this point, the other barges started to back away and eventually vanished from view. To the French, it obviously seemed like another attempt to outflank them and this is what their accounts tell.

It was, in fact, something quite different which, once again, had gone wrong for the British. The young engineer, Lt. Clerk, had been looking for suitable sites to install artillery batteries and, on the morning of the 8th, he found a good spot. It was a fine spot at the foot of Rattlesnake Mountain, probably on a flat clear space which was conveniently covered by an earthen bluff on the west side which would protect it from the French guns in Fort Carillon. About a kilometer away, in front of the British battery was the side of the entrenchments on the heights of Ticonderoga

It seemed perfect, and Clerk organized guns, gunners, ammunition and barges with some battoemen to carry it all to the chosen spot and put up the battery. Around noon the barges set off, seemingly at the same time as the first attacks on the entrenchments. The men guiding the barges then made a fatal mistake, or perhaps were carried too quickly by the strong current. When they came to the large island, they kept edging the north shore of the river instead of veering to its southern side in order to land at the chosen site. In keeping to the north shore, they soon came into full view of the French fort and its artillery fire. Under bombardment, with some of the equipment sunk and the surviving men surely confused and shaken, the idea of the battery was put aside. It was, in retrospect, a serious omission for the British not to try again, but, in the heat of successive assaults, the priorities must have altered.

IN THE LINE OF FIRE

On the heights of Ticonderoga, the British were not about to give up. Repeatedly repulsed, they kept re-forming and went back in with great courage and stubbornness. Capt. Desandrouin, now that his engineer's duties were over, served Montcalm as a temporary ADC, checking how the men were holding up against the attacks and give them news of successes elsewhere. Such news cheered them greatly and they would shout "Vive le roi!" (long live the king!) or "Vive notre général!" (hail our general!). Several times, Montcalm sent him along the lines to inquire if they needed assistance, reported Desandrouin, but the men always told him "we don't need help here," adding that he should see if help was needed elsewhere. The men's main worry, "even the veteran soldiers," was that the Anglo-Americans would outflank them from either side of the entrenchments.

Montcalm too was there among his men. He had taken his coat off, as it was a hot day, and kept encouraging his soldiers, making sure that detachments of grenadiers and piquets were sent to reinforce and give heart to the men in the line wherever they seemed threatened. He was at his best here, a brave and energetic battlefield commander who had a quick eye for any crisis, who loved sharing the dangers with his men, who managed to keep control and who could lead coolly in the heat of battle. The same battlefield leadership qualities were not shared by his opponent, however.

Pouchot reported a curious incident when an excited Capt. Bassignac of Royal-Roussillon tied his red handkerchief to the end of his musket and waved it triumphantly over the entrenchment wall – but this was mistaken as a sign for quarter by the British, red being the "English color". Desandrouin was also told of this tragic incident which occurred where the Guyenne battalion was posted. A number of British soldiers were seen to come up waving their hats and shouting "bon quartier!" (quarter!) thinking the French were surrendering. The soldiers of

Although it does not seem like a height, just beyond the trees, with remnants of the entrenchment, the ground falls. (Photo: RC)

Guyenne, somewhat confused, thought the British soldiers were wanting to surrender and shouted back "armes bas" (weapons down) and stopped firing. According to Desandrouin, who heard the story from British officers after the battle, it was the flags of the Guyenne battalion (see accompanying illustration) being waved by the ensigns every time the men shouted "Vive le roi!" rather than the red handkerchief which caused the confusion. In any event, Pouchot arrived on the spot to find the French "soldiers perched on top of the retrenchments" and noted at the same time "the forward movement of the enemy." He immediately shouted to the soldiers: "Fire, fire; Can't you see that these troops are going to overrun your position?" This "suddenly brought the soldiers to their senses and, still standing, they fired a volley, shooting down two or three hundred of them." The French volleys were later denounced as treachery, but it was a fatal case of mistaken interpretations.

The most stubborn attacks were usually at the center, but the British soldiers' outstanding bravery did not waver. Time after time, units went up, struggled across the *abbatis,* now strewn with mangled bodies, and were shot at close range. The French soldiers were just as resolute. Malartic noted that "our soldiers were so attached to their place, that I could not have two to go get cartridges which were starting to run out." He was forced to order two sergeants to accompany him to the rear to get a case of cartridges. According to Desandrouin, it had been "impossible to find more coolness and bravery than were seen of soldiers that day. I witnessed that none fired without aiming at his man, and that most waited, sometime rather a long time, to see a skirmisher show himself

Inside the French entrenchments the log walls protected the French soldiers firing on the attacking Anglo-American troops. The fusiliers at the wall were selected from the better shots; loaded muskets were passed to them or they might load with only ball and powder when rapid fire was required; at other times, they took aimed shots at enemy sharpshooters in the *abbatis*. Behind in reserve were the battalion's grenadiers and piquets ready to intervene should the attackers manage to break in. The battalion's HQ was to be marked by the two battalion colors but, at Ticonderoga, at least one of these was at the log wall. The three sectors of the French position were commanded by Bourlamarque on the right, Lévis on the left and Montcalm at the center. The sector that came under the most intense assault by the 42nd Highlanders in the late afternoon of 8 July was defended by Royal-Roussillon. Montcalm went there with some reserves to check any breach in the position. He wore a waistcoat that day, possibly his gold-laced scarlet general's waistcoat. An officer of the metropolitan army engineers, most likely Desandrouin, in blue and red is at Montcalm's right and an officer of Royal-Roussillon at his left. A drummer would have been nearby and possibly a Canadian militiaman for communication with the colonial troops and militias posted on the northern flank. The French soldiers at the log wall probably took their waistcoats off but kept wearing their grey-white coat to avoid confusion as had been done during the Fort William-Henry campaign the previous summer.

The field north of the fort is still clear of trees. On 8 July 1758, gunners in the fort fired a few shots at Canadian militiamen fleeing across the field; this convinced them to get back to their lines. (Photo: RC)

from behind a log, so as not miss him, in spite of the hail of bullets ..." The British and American casualties were already high, but the French too were being shot at. Between the attacking columns were rangers and light infantrymen taking cover and firing at the loopholes and heads or hats showing over the entrenchment walls. As some of the skirmishers were armed with rifles, their marksmanship must have been especially effective and resulted in many head wounds which were often fatal. Another cause of casualties, which appears to have affected the grenadiers and piquets in particular, were the masses of British bullets which arced over the men in the entrenchment, but hit those further back in reserve.

The New England provincial troops were called upon from about 2 pm to reinforce the British regulars. The rearguard of Connecticut, Rhode Island and New Jersey troops was marched up to join the Massachusetts regiments and support the regulars' renewed attacks. They seem to have formed themselves between the regular brigades, but however they formed, they went in and also suffered severe casualties. Such troops could not be expected to have the same determination as the British regulars but it was hoped they might run up to and climb the entrenchments. They had no more success than the regulars, but certainly did not lack courage either. One William Smith, a private in Babcock's Rhode Island Regiment, became something of a local hero when the American press later published his feats. He actually managed to get to the bottom of the entrenchment wall and shoot several French soldiers before one above realized he was there. The French soldier fired down on Smith, wounding him but the aggressive Rhode Islander mustered enough strength to strike him with his tomahawk, escape and live to tell the tale.

From about 2.30 pm, the British attacks decreased as Gen. Abercromby called back his mauled regiments to regroup and recuperate. Once again, his instructions were badly relayed or ignored. Grant's brigade, consisting of the 42nd and 46th, continued to stage new attacks, for example. It seems that others joined them too and the shooting kept on, punctuated by various surges into the afternoon. As a result, Col. Bourlamarque commanding the French right was wounded at about 4 pm Lieutenant-colonels Sénézergues of La Sarre and Privat of Languedoc replaced him and continued "giving the best orders" according to La Pause.

Bougainville noted that the *abbatis* in front of the entrenchment caught fire several times during the battle, but were always promptly put out thanks to "soldiers courageously passing over" the log wall. Men from Berry's 3rd Battalion were mostly young recruits, generally considered less able to stand firm, and had been posted in Fort Carillon. However, some were detached to the entrenchments at the heights and proved very useful carrying ammunition and water to the soldiers at the log walls during the many hours of fighting.

THE BLACK WATCH'S DESPERATE ATTACK

Legend has it that three years before the battle, in the Western Highlands of Scotland, a man asked Maj. Duncan Campbell of Inverawe, 42nd Foot, for shelter, admitting that he had killed a man in a fray. Campbell took him to a nearby cave and swore on his dirk not to expose him. Campbell went home to find that his foster brother had been killed. Bound by his oath, Campbell said nothing. That night, the blood-smeared ghost of his foster brother appeared at his bedside and uttered: "Inverawe! Inverawe! Blood has been shed. Shield not the murderer!" When Campbell went to the cave, the stranger was gone. The next night, the vision appeared again, ghastly pale, and said: "Farewell, Inverawe! Farewell, till we meet at Ticonderoga!" and vanished. Years passed, and Campbell's regiment went to America. The strange name uttered by the ghost was recognized with horror by Campbell when the 42nd was ordered to be part of the army attacking Ticonderoga.

Charge of the 42nd Highlanders at Ticonderoga according to a British print of 1884.

BATTLE OF TICONDEROGA, 8 JULY 1758 1300–1900 HRS

Phase 5 – From 1400 hrs: New England provincial troops in reserve are sent to join the attacking columns.

6

6

2

1

5

D

5

C

3

5

B

A

TICONDEROGA

I

8

LA CHUTE RIVER

7

8

Phase 4 – About 1400 hrs–1430 hrs: British barges with cannons come down La Chute River but they mistakenly take the north channel and come into view of Fort Carillon. The Cannoniers-Bombardiers gunners in the fort open up the barges, sink a few and the rest turn back.

ANGLO-AMERICAN UNITS

1 Columns attacking the French left (initially 42nd and 44th, later mixed)
2 Columns attacking the French centre (initially 46th and 55th, later mixed)
3 Column attacking south of the French left (42nd and 44th)
4 Columns attacking the French right (initially 60th, grenadiers and New York regiment; later assaults included the most determined attack of the 42nd with 46th and grenadiers at about 1700 hrs)
5 Rangers, Armed Battoemen and 80th Light Infantry (skirmishers in the abbatis)
6 Connecticut and Rhode Island provincial regiments (join in the attacking columns from 1400 hrs)
7 British barges laden with artillery
8 Mohawk Indians

FRENCH UNITS

A La Sarre (Bourlamarque's La Sarre Brigade)
B Languedoc (Bourlamarque's La Sarre Brigade)
C 2/Berry (Montcalm's Royal-Roussillon Brigade)
D Royal-Roussillon (Montcalm's Royal-Roussillon Brigade)
E La Reine (Lévis' La Reine Brigade)
F Béarn (Lévis' La Reine Brigade)
G Guyenne (Lévis' La Reine Brigade)
H *Compagnies franches de la Marine* and Canadian Militia
I Duprat's and Bernard's volunteer companies
J 3/Berry
K *Canonniers-Bombardiers* attending batteries in Fort Carillon

XX

MONTCALM

Phase 3 – About 1400 hrs: A British column (42nd and 44th) tries to outflank the French left; they run into Duprat's and Bernard's volunteers and the Royal-Roussillon detachments. La Sarre and Guyenne in the entrenchments take the British in cross-fire and the British column retreats.

XXX

ABERCROMBY

Phase 1 – **1330-1900 hrs: This is the continuous phase of this battle from early afternoon to early evening. All the Anglo-American assaults, no matter how gallant, are repulsed by the defenders.**

Phase 8 – **About 1700–1830 hrs: The 42nd Highlanders make a strong assault on the French right, a few even get into the French position but the attack fails as does another on the centre. By 1900 hrs, the Anglo-American army withdraws from the Ticonderoga heights covered by its light infantrymen.**

4
4
4
F
G
H
H
H
H

FORT CARILLON

K

J

LAKE CHAMPLAIN

N

Phase 7 – **Late afternoon: French colonial troops go into the woods and skirmish the British column attacking the French right.**

Phase 6 – **Mid to late afternoon: British assaults continue, especially against the French left and centre. French Brigadier Bourlamarque is badly wounded at about 1600 hrs and replaced by battalion commanders; French position holds steady.**

Phase 2 – **About 1345 hrs: Some Canadian militiamen panic and start to run away. Canonniers-Bombardiers, colonial artillerymen, spot this and fire at the militiamen; startled, they go back to their positions.**

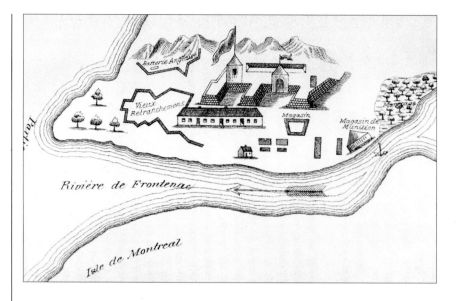

The night before the battle, a gloomy Campbell said he was sure to die and in the final hours of the battle, his foreboding was proved to be correct.

Sometime before 5 pm, a massive and desperate attack was staged by two columns united into one which included the 42nd and the grenadiers. The 42nd was the most numerous regiment in Abercromby's army and the utter bravery and tenacity of the Highlanders in an attack was renowned. They attacked the French right defended by La Reine, Béarn and Guyenne who, sensing this was the critical point of the battle, gave it all they could. The Highlanders in particular seemed almost unstoppable, in spite of grievous losses. "Even those that were mortally wounded, cried aloud to their companions, not to mind or lose a thought for them, but to follow their officers, and charge the enemy, and to mind the honor of their king and country. Nay, their ardor was so very extraordinary, that they could not be brought off while they had a single shot remaining," wrote Lt. William Grant. Montcalm noted especially the column "of grenadiers and Scottish Highlanders, which always charged again, without breaking or hesitation, and several were killed within fifteen paces" of the French entrenchments.

A few Highlanders actually managed, with some luck and a great deal of sheer heroism, to get beyond the sharp branches of the *abbatis* to the foot of the entrenchment wall. Led by Capt. John Campbell, they climbed it and leapt among the French soldiers, no doubt slashing right and left with their long Highland broadswords. According to La Pause, there had also been a vigorous assault on the center defended by Royal-Roussillon and Berry, and the Highlanders attacking the French right then moved to the center "so that the danger became very great in this part." It would seem that this is about when and where some of the Highlanders came over the entrenchments. However, the "Chevalier de Lévis went there with some troops from the [French] right which the enemy was only shooting at; the Marquis de Montcalm ran there also with a few reserve troops and the enemy" did not stand a chance. The Highlanders were immediately bayoneted, probably by the grenadiers in reserve who were waiting for just such an occasion. The British, La Pause went on, were now "meeting resistance which at last slowed their ardor."

SKIRMISHERS AND FINAL ATTACKS

Another factor which must have affected the Anglo-Americans was that they were being skirmished by parties of colonial troops from the French right. The colonial infantrymen and Canadian militiamen posted just beyond the *abbatis* had not been attacked and Lévis, commanding the French right sector, had earlier ordered them to go ahead from their position to the woods and skirmish the British. This was not immediately obeyed according to Lévis, the militiamen being especially hesitant, but eventually parties were in the woods peppering the British. The column of the 42nd and 46th reacted unflinchingly; some men detached from it and opened fire on the skirmishers who retreated, but kept harassing from a distance. In the late afternoon, 255 colonial troops arrived from Saint-Frédéric and "a great part of them went to the battlefield," said Montcalm.

At about 6 pm the British columns tried again to storm the French right, then the center and finally the left, without any further success. Indeed the attacks were slackening as the Anglo-Americans finally realized they could not overcome Montcalm's position. Around 7 pm they retreated from the battlefield, covered by the light troops.

According to Lt. Grant of the 42nd, his regiment had "paid dearly for their intrepidity" as nearly half its officers and men were killed or wounded. However, the "remains of the regiment had the honor to cover the retreat of the army, and brought off the wounded." This was not the case in every sector, for La Pause remarked that the dead and some of the wounded were left behind. Bougainville observed as much, stating that at "seven o'clock the enemy thought only of retreat, covered by the fire of their light troops." Malartic noted that the order to cease fire was given about then, when it was realized the Anglo-American skirmishers were only firing isolated shots as they were retreating.

Montcalm cheered by his troops following the final repulse of the British assaults on 8 July 1758. Many of the uniform details are erroneous in this early-20th-century painting by Henry Ogden, but it captures marvelously well the elation in the French camp after the battle. (Fort Ticonderoga Museum)

Of the many courageous charges made by British and New England troops against the French entrenchments, in the afternoon of 8 July 1758, the most determined and ferocious were made by the brave Highlanders of the 42nd Regiment (The Black Watch). Time and again, they persisted in their attacks, hoping to find a weak spot in the French log wall. Some were seen in a rage hacking away at the *abbatis* before them; the wounded encouraged their comrades to attack rather than help them; some few even managed to climb up the log wall and jump into the French position wielding their broadswords, meeting their end bayoneted by French soldiers. The casualties resulting from such outstanding conduct under fire were terrible: some 647 were reported killed, wounded or lost, well over half of the regiment.

AFTERMATH

ABERCROMBY WITHDRAWS

So ended the bloody battle of Ticonderoga. Had there been many Indians with Montcalm, the British and New Englanders' retreat might have been more complicated. As things stood, all French accounts agree that their officers and men were exhausted and a pursuit was out of the question. Indeed, Montcalm and Lévis were very aware that Abercromby might try again at dawn on 9 July. The whole French army stayed at the entrenchments, the soldiers cleaned their muskets and slept there, the night being warm and clear, punctuated by the moaning of the badly wounded scattered all over the *abbatis*.

Sir Jeffery Amherst, General in Chief of the British forces in North America in 1759, led the army which finally forced the French to withdraw from Ticonderoga that year.
(Print after Sir Joshua Reynolds)

Lake Champlain from Fort Ticonderoga as seen by Henry James Warre, a British tourist who visited the site in 1842. A few overgrown stones can be seen in the foreground. Warre, from the famous Port House family, was the son of William Warre who had been Marshal Beresford's ADC during the Peninsular War. (National Archives of Canada, C31270)

In the French camp 9 July began in much the same way as the previous day, the drummers beating "*La Générale*" at the crack of dawn, the piquets out in front of the *abbatis*. The first concern was to refurbish the entrenchments and finish off the lines and the batteries. A party of volunteers went out towards the Anglo-American army's position and found the temporary entrenchments they had made about half-way between the heights and the bridge at the saw mills abandoned and Abercromby's army gone. Word was brought back to the French lines upon which soldiers went into the *abbatis* to carry out the remaining wounded British soldiers. As there were no Indians with the French army to provide further intelligence on the Anglo-Americans, it was decided to spend the day repairing and finishing the various field works. The French believed that Abercromby had suffered about 4,000 casualties, but with 16,000–21,000 men remaining, he might try again, this time with artillery. By evening, most of the works had progressed considerably with trenches now crossing the length of the peninsula.

On 10 July there was still no sign of Anglo-American movement. Montcalm therefore assigned the companies of grenadiers, the volunteers of Duprat and Bernard, and 100 Canadian militiamen to go out under Gen. Lévis to find Abercromby's force. On the way to the saw mills, Lévis found some more wounded, who were brought back to the French lines. Once there, he split his force "going by different ways": one party edged the La Chute River and the other followed the Portage

Road, until they all reached the northern end of Lake George. There he found "the remains of an hurried retreat," and recovered all that could be useful, including scores of "flour barrels which had been thrown in the water". Detachments were sent as far as about 12 km south, who confirmed the Anglo-American army was gone.

CONFLICTING CASUALTY COUNTS

On 11 July the dead were buried. This included "about 800" British or New England soldiers found dead by Montcalm's men or who had died of wounds in the French hospitals. As this figure is in Lévis' journal, a man not prone to much exaggeration, the figure is worth retaining. Writing to William Pitt the next day, Abercromby computed "464 regulars killed, 69 missing, 1,117 wounded and 87 provincials killed, eight missing and 239 wounded" including officers. This makes 628 killed or missing, which was bad enough but he could not have had information as to the fate of many others including those who died later in the French camp. It is thus obvious that Abercromby must have considerably minimized the actual figure. If the French buried some 800 men, these were only the bodies they found and did not include all the dead and mortally wounded that were brought back to the British lines during the battle. The number of officers killed must have been the figure of 34 as given by Abercromby, but the number of enlisted men killed, regulars or provincials, would have been

The remains of Fort Crown Point. Gen. Amherst ordered this substantial fort built in 1759 as protection against a possible French counterattack. A few years later, Lord Adam Gordon noted that it was "built in a most masterly manner. It has five bastions, mounts 105 guns, and has casemates for 4000 men." The stone walls of the quarters (left) and the main men's barracks (right) are preserved. (Photo: RC)

HUDSON BAY

RUPERT'S LAND

HUDSON'S BAY COMPANY

NEWFOUNDLAND

St Lawrence

To Quebec

Gulf of
St Lawrence

F R A N C E

C A N A D A

ACADIA

Île
St Jean

Louisbourg
Île Royale

Quebec

Montreal

Halifax
NOVA
SCOTIA

Lake Superior

Lake
Huron

Lake Michigan

Frontenac

Ticonderoga

Lake Ontario

Niagara

Detroit

Lake Erie

Albany

Boston

N E W

Ohio

New York
Philadelphia

BRITISH
COLONIES

L O U I S I A N A

Ohio

Mississippi

Williamsburg

ATLANTIC
OCEAN

New Orleans

FLORIDA

GULF OF MEXICO

BAHAMA
ISLANDS

N

CUBA

MEXICO

HISPANOLIA

HAITI

	Britain
	France
	Spain
	Disputed
←	British attacks

0   250 miles
0   400 km

much higher; perhaps as many as 1,000 or more actually perished. The reported wounded were probably much the same, if perhaps marginally more. A reasonable estimate might be about 1,000 killed and missing, and 1,500 wounded for a total of 2,500 casualties for the battle of 8 July. When added to the casualties incurred on 6 July, consisting of about 100 killed and wounded including two officers, the figure would be about 2,600 for the campaign.

The French casualties were naturally considerably less, but nevertheless quite high for an army which could ill afford any losses. For Montcalm's army the action on 6 July was painful, resulting in the loss of Trépezec and five other officers, as well as some 300 men killed, wounded or made prisoners. On 9 July, Lévis reported that the loss on 8 July had been 14 officers and 92 men killed, 18 officers and 248 men wounded for a total of 372 casualties. These figures were revised slightly later, and the official account published in France in December mentioned 12 officers and 92 men killed, 25 officers and 248 men wounded for a total of 377 casualties. When added to the casualties of 6 July, the total comes to some 527 for the campaign although one can estimate it was more like 554.

Montcalm's casualty rate was some 13 percent of his army. Abercromby's, official figure was only 11.5 percent, but in reality was more like 15 percent or so. Another way to calculate percentage is according to the number of men actually engaged in the battle which might have been about 3,700 for Montcalm and perhaps 10,000 or 12,000 for Abercromby. But all these calculations seem, in the end, somewhat futile when one reflects on the grief brought to thousands of wives, daughters, sons, parents, and friends of so many fine and brave men.

RECRIMINATION AND COVER-UPS

The battle of 8 July was a tremendous pounding match by all-out frontal assaults. All had failed. It was singular in that there was no serious British attempt to outflank or even to create a diversion. The artillery, which had been so painstakingly brought this far into the wilderness, was not deployed at all except for one timid and failed attempt. Strong counter lines of entrenchments could have been built by the British to secure their position and seal in the French on the peninsula. None of this was done. The considerable four-to-one advantages of numbers enjoyed by Abercromby was all gambled on the assaults in a matter of hours.

The French defense, if most gallant, could hardly be called innovative. Here too, there had been no real thought to create a diversion other than Levis' attempt to send out colonial troops and Canadians to skirmish the flanks of British columns. It might be argued that Montcalm could have planned to fully use his colonial troops to harass the flanks and rear of the enemy force. However, Montcalm was never too keen on the Canadian tactics of woodland warfare and besides, he knew the British had a large and competent force of light infantry to oppose such a move. Leaving daring moves aside, he thought it better to keep those colonial troops to cover his own flank which turned out to be a fairly static role.

The subsequent letters show that Abercromby decided to shoulder the blame, while claiming he had been badly advised by his young chief

Fort Crown Point's earthen and timber walls and bastions, built from 1759, remain in surprisingly good shape and are now a protected New York State historic site. The south wall and the magazine bastion below the men's barracks can be seen. (Photo: RC)

engineer, Lt. Clerk, who was conveniently killed in the field on 8 July. This was also a worthy covering operation, for it whitewashed Bradstreet who came up with similar erroneous information, protected Rogers, who did not provide the skirmisher screen he was supposed to, and absolved Haviland, who independently decided to engage his column. Brigade commander Grant was not above reproach either, as he stubbornly maintained his Highlanders' attacks after Abercromby had asked for withdrawal to regroup. And most of all, Gage, the absent and unseen second-in-command who appears to have contributed very little. The subterfuge worked, as most of the officers went on to promotions and distinguished careers, particularly Gage.

Montcalm's day of glory was widely publicized in France and his flush reports of his victory gave no credit to the colonial troops. Indeed, he minimized their numbers and role. As a result, Governor-General Vaudreuil wrote in August to the minister of the navy that the colonial troops had "nearly blown up and if the worse [a mutiny] did not happen, it was due to their spirit of moderation. And their mortification was great when they saw that M. de Montcalm, instead of reporting their services, attributed them to the metropolitan troops." It seems a pity that Montcalm did not use the opportunity to try to bind together the two rival camps in his army as a result of this remarkable victory; but true to his volatile character, he did exactly the contrary. Only after his death at Quebec, in September 1759 (see the book by the same author, *Order Of Battle 3: Quebec 1759*, Osprey, 1999), when Lévis assumed command was an attempt made to unify the army.

THE BATTLEFIELD TODAY

In 1759 Gen. Amherst marched on Ticonderoga with another large army and Bourlamarque, who commanded the small French force, evacuated the area, blowing up both Fort Carillon and Fort Saint-Frédéric. The British repaired Fort Carillon, renaming it Fort Ticonderoga, and built a large new fort at Crown Point. Ticonderoga was captured by the American revolutionaries in 1775 and reoccupied by the British in 1777. Thereafter, the fort was abandoned and the battle site, once a clear field, gradually became overgrown.

Today, the low mounds which form the remains of the line of entrenchments on the heights of Ticonderoga, are in the middle of a forest of tall trees. Here and there, are a few monuments including a tall cross, a reproduction of one erected by Montcalm to commemorate the victory, and a fine stone memorial to the Black Watch in remembrance of its heroism.

Thanks to the efforts of Stephen Pell and the continuing support of his descendants and of many friends, the whole area is now a fine park with the restored Fort Ticonderoga as its centerpiece. No matter where one stands on its walls and bastions, the view is majestic.

The September 1908 clambake at Ticonderoga hosted by the Ticonderoga Historical Society. It was at this event that the decision was taken to restore the fort and preserve the adjacent grounds. (Fort Ticonderoga Museum)

Stephen H. P. Pell (1874–1950) was the driving force behind the restoration of Fort Ticonderoga and the preservation of its battlefield. He started in the fall of 1908 with the help of Alfred Bossom, a young British architect, later to become Lord Bossom of Maidstone. Pell, a naval veteran of the Spanish-American war, served with the ambulances in the French and later the American army during World War I. He lived to see his decades of careful and determined work become one of America's best-known and best-loved national monuments. He is shown in a French army chasseur uniform. (Fort Ticonderoga Museum)

That single battle, be it Carillon or Ticonderoga, still has a romantic aura today, as indeed it has since the 19th century. The superb scenic beauty of the area – forest-covered mountains and lovely lakes – would dwarf large armies even now as it certainly did in the 18th century. For the British, the Scots and the Americans, it was testimony to an outstanding display of desperate bravery and stubborn heroism in the face of enormous obstacles against a worthy enemy. For the French and the French Canadians, it became a vindication of battlefield prowess through a stunning victory over overwhelming odds of four to one, a triumphant day with flag waving, before the defeats and capitulations at Quebec and Montreal the following years. Thus, to this day, many towns in Quebec have their "Carillon" and "Montcalm" streets in memory of a ray of hope and a dash of glory from desperate times long past.

CHRONOLOGY

1609 **30 July** French explorer Samuel de Champlain arrives in the Ticonderoga area, and scatters Iroquois warriors in battle.

1731 French fort at Crown Point started, eventually named Fort Saint-Frédéric.

1755 **8 July** Gen. Braddock's British army defeated at the Monongahela by French and Indians.

8 September French army under Gen. Dieskau repulsed by an army of New Englanders under Sir William Johnson at the southern end of Lake George.

20 September Fort Carillon ordered built at Ticonderoga by Governor-General Vaudreuil of New France. Work starts in mid-October under the direction of engineer de Lobtinière.

1756 **13 May** The Marquis de Montcalm lands in Quebec to assume command of the French army in Canada.

10–14 August Siege and capture of Fort Oswego by Montcalm.

1757 **3–6 August** Siege and capture of Fort William-Henry by Montcalm.

30 December British Prime Minister William Pitt names Gen. Abercromby as commander-in-chief, and instructs him to attack Ticonderoga. News received at Albany on 7 March 1758.

1758 **Late June** Abercromby's army gathers at southern end of Lake George; Montcalm's army at Ticonderoga.

30 June Montcalm arrives at Ticonderoga.

5 July Abercromby's army embarks to cross Lake George.

6 July Abercromby's army lands at northern end of Lake George, runs into lost French column at Bernetz Brook, Lord Howe killed in engagement.

7 July Abercromby's army nears Ticonderoga via the Portage Road. Montcalm's army builds entrenchments and *abbatis* on Ticonderoga heights.

8 July Battle of Ticonderoga.

9 July Abercromby's army withdraws to southern end of Lake George.

1759 **26 July** French forces blow up Fort Carillon and withdraw before Gen. Amherst's vastly superior Anglo-American army.

August 1 French forces blow up Fort Saint-Frédéric at Crown Point and withdraw before Amherst's army.

September British make some repairs to Fort Carillon, rename it Fort Ticonderoga and post a small garrison.

13 September Battle of the Plains of Abraham in Quebec, generals Montcalm and Wolfe killed.

1760 **8 September** Gen. Lévis surrenders with French army at Montreal to Gen. Amherst's British and New England army.

1763 Peace between France and Britain ends Seven Years War. Canada ceded to Great Britain.

1775 **April** Outbreak of American Revolution.

9 May Fort Ticonderoga captured from the British in a daring surprise raid by Ethan Allen and the Green Mountain Boys.

1777 **5 July** Fort Ticonderoga abandoned by Americans to British forces under Gen. Burgoyne; never used again as a garrison.

1783 End of War of American Independence,

FURTHER READING

There is a fair body of various writings in English regarding Ticonderoga. The history of the fort has been covered in Edward P. Hamilton's *Fort Ticonderoga: Key to a Continent* (Boston, 1964, republished by Fort Ticonderoga in 1995) which basically takes the interpretation of the battle as found in Francis Parkman's classic but dated *Montcalm and Wolfe* (1884 and countless reprints).

Many useful items on the troops, personalities and forts of the area are in Alan Gallay, ed., *Colonial Wars of North America 1512–1763: An Encyclopedia* (New York & London, 1996) and the various biographies in the *Dictionary of Canadian Biography* (Toronto, Vols. 3 and 4, 1974–1980). R. Chartrand's Vols. 1 and 2 of *Canadian Military Heritage* (Montreal, 1993 and 1995) has various data regarding the French troops not found elsewhere, as do *Louis XV's Army (2) French Infantry* (Osprey MAA 302) and *Louis XV's Army (5) Colonial and Naval Troops* (MAA 313). American provincial troops are especially well studied in Fred Anderson's *A People's Army: Massachusetts Soldiers and Society in the Seven Years War* (Chappel Hill, North Carolina, 1984), Harold F. Selesky's *War & Society in Colonial Connecticut* (New Haven, 1990) and Douglas Leach's *Arms for Empire: a Military History of the British Colonies in North America 1607–1775* (New York, 1973). There is also a sizable amount written in French, of which we will only cite here H.R. Casgain's *Montcalm et Lévis* (Tours, 1898, and reprints).

Published primary sources are numerous in English concerning the British and Americans, thanks in particular to the admirable *Bulletin of the Fort Ticonderoga Museum* which has been publishing journals and contemporary correspondence related to Ticonderoga for the past half-century. The documents edited by Nicholas Westbrook and Ian McCulloch in Vol. XVI, No. 1 (1998) are especially recommended. Curiously, the senior British commanders left no journals. Edmund O'Callaghan, ed., *Documents Relative to the Colonial History of the State of New York*, especially Vol. X (Albany, 1858, the full series recently republished as CDs) reproduces key British and French documents in English. Various letters are found isolated in a host of other publications requiring a full bibliography; for instance, Major Eyre's letter of 10 July 1758 is in Stanley Pargelli's *Military Affairs in North America 1748–1765* (New York, 1936). *Adventure in the Wilderness: The American Journals of Louis Antoine de Bougainville*, translated and edited by Edward P. Hamilton (Norman, 1964), Pierre Pouchot, *Memoirs of the Late War in North America,* translated by Michael Cardy and edited by Brian Leigh Dunnigan (Fort Niagara, 1994) and the 1929 *Report of the Public Archives of Canada* contain translations of Montcalm's letters, essential for those who read solely English. There are also a large number of documents published only in French, such as the journals of Montcalm, Lévis,

Malartic, Desandrouin and La Pause, all of whom played important parts on the Ticonderoga campaign.

Many other documents are unpublished in various archives. In France, Archives Nationales, Colonies (located in Aix), series C11A, Vols 100 to 104 and the Service Historique de l'Armée de Terre, Archives de la Guerre (located at the Château of Vincennes), series A1, Vol. 3457 in particular. Various volumes in Britain's Public Records Office (Kew) in WO 1 and WO 34 have British and American correspondence. The National (formerly Public) Archives of Canada have the papers of Bourlamarque and Bradstreet, and the Fort Ticonderoga Museum has more unpublished journals of the campaign.

INDEX

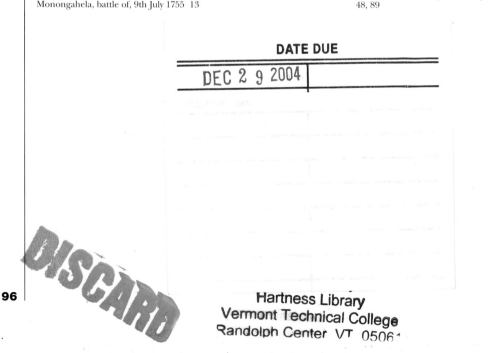

DATE DUE

DEC 2 9 2004

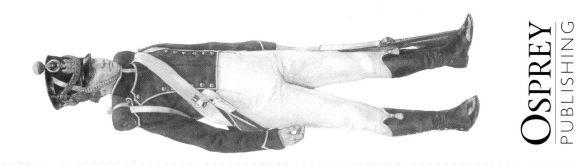

FIND OUT MORE ABOUT OSPREY

❏ Please send me the latest listing of Osprey's publications

❏ I would like to subscribe to Osprey's e-mail newsletter

Title / rank _____

Name _____

Address _____

_____

City / county _____

Postcode / zip _____ state / country _____

e-mail _____

I am interested in:

❏ Ancient world
❏ Medieval world
❏ 16th century
❏ 17th century
❏ 18th century
❏ Napoleonic
❏ 19th century

❏ American Civil War
❏ World War 1
❏ World War 2
❏ Modern warfare
❏ Military aviation
❏ Naval warfare

Please send to:

USA & Canada:
Osprey Direct USA, c/o MBI Publishing, P.O. Box 1, 729 Prospect Avenue, Osceola, WI 54020

UK, Europe and rest of world:
Osprey Direct UK, P.O. Box 140, Wellingborough, Northants, NN8 2FA, United Kingdom

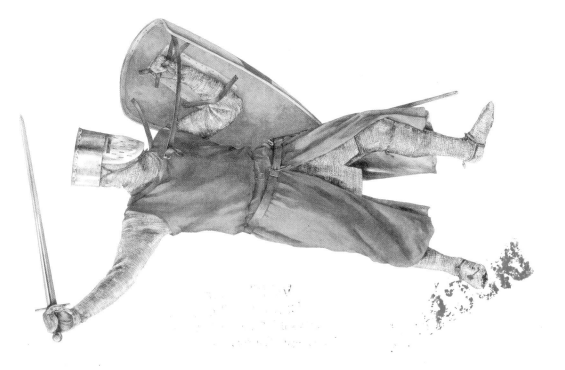

www.ospreypublishing.com

call our telephone hotline
for a free information pack

USA & Canada: 1-800-826-6600
UK, Europe and rest of world call:
+44 (0) 1933 443 863

Young Guardsman
Figure taken from *Warrior 22:*
Imperial Guardsman 1799–1815
Published by Osprey
Illustrated by Christa Hook

Knight, c.1190
Figure taken from *Warrior 1: Norman Knight 950 – 1204 AD*
Published by Osprey
Illustrated by Christa Hook

POSTCARD